"In The Proper Pursuit, Bill Cripe tackles a sensitive subject in a clear, bold, biblical manner. His message may not prove particularly popular in this self-indulgent age, but it's a necessary one. Thank God for his courage to write. It's now up to every one of us to read and heed."

Daryl E. Witmer
Executive director
AIIA Institute

"Cripe provides us with a balanced, biblically-guided critique of those he sees as some of its leading proponents, as well as the dangers that are inherent in presenting the gospel in this way. Bill helps his readers understand why this is a "different" gospel and why it is such an important issue for the church in our day. This is recommended reading for anyone pursuing truth."

Keith Tolley
President
Vision New England

D1743496

The

PROPER
PURSUIT *of*
PROSPERITY

WILLIAM E. CRIPE, SR.

The
PROPER
PURSUIT *of*
PROSPERITY

Balancing the Promises of Heaven
with the Experiences of Earth

TATE PUBLISHING & *Enterprises*

Published by Tate Publishing & Enterprises, LLC
127 E. Trade Center Terrace | Mustang, Oklahoma 73064 USA
1.888.361.9473 | www.tatepublishing.com

Tate Publishing is committed to excellence in the publishing industry. The company reflects the philosophy established by the founders, based on Psalm 68:11,
"The Lord gave the word and great was the company of those who published it."

Book design copyright © 2011 by Tate Publishing, LLC. All rights reserved.
Cover design by Amber Gulilat
Interior design by Chelsea Womble
Author Photo by Jane Veilleux

Published in the United States of America

ISBN: 978-1-61346-101-3
1. Religion, Faith
2. Religion, Christian Ministry, Evangelism
11.07.05

DEDICATION

To Barbara, high school sweetheart, love of my life, human source of my strength, and the confidant of my soul. Forever, For always, No matter what.

And for you, Mom, for building into me the confidence to tackle anything.

ACKNOWLEDGMENTS

Any book is a collaborative effort. Without the spirit-filled generosity and partnership of Keith and Millie Tolley, I might still be chiseling away at the cost of my seminary education. Their inspiring "openness" took me from the dark basement of endeavor to the light of His success.

From our spiritual infancy, Tim and Jan Arensmeier and Bob and Amy Jones were our living examples of what Jesus was like and what He wanted us to be. Their lives were used by God, developing within me and my wife a real faith while seeing that living for Christ, and having fun doing it, are both possible.

My gratitude to the Amy Foundation, whose honoring me with my first writing award made me pause to consider that I could truly write. By my fourth award, I had the compulsion to pursue a book.

It is with humility that I say, "Thank you," to the folks at Tate Publishing for seeing past the roughness of a draft and for seeing something worth pursuing. Sabrina, thank you for your gentleness and encouragement in the editorial process.

My conviction to write on this subject was born out of the inspiration gleaned in the two decades as chief shepherd of the faithful, loving, and generous congregation of Faith Evangelical Free Church. The small rural church, which began in a converted duplex, is a living example of what God's people can do when living in light of the proper pursuit of prosperity. Special thanks to Sally Foster, Dave Jarvis, and the staff of Faith EFC for carrying my load while I worked on this book during sabbatical and to CMB, who may never know the power of those words: "Write the book!"

To the glory of God, I truly give thanks to the multitude of unknown benefactors whose generosity in Jesus's name have blessed my family with so much more than a Spartan existence, gracing us with the bounty of life's pleasures.

Finally, thank you Tanis for showing the family at Faith what God's grace and a proper pursuit of prosperity looks like. Through the intractable pain of incurable cancer, you wear suffering like a jeweled gown reflecting the One in whose image and likeness you have been made. The reason the visage you see in that mirror does not look like you is because now you look like your Father.

May the Lord Jesus magnify His name and deliver all His hurting and beleaguered loved ones who are in bondage to the tantalizing sway of the prosperity gospel.

TABLE OF CONTENTS

INTRODUCTION

My wife and I were young when the encyclopedia salesman dropped by the house. The deal he presented seemed too good to be true. I know, I know! An alarm should have gone off, but remember, I said we were young. He was going to give us a complete set of new encyclopedias—*free*. I know, I know. Show him the door, right? Did I say we were young?

By the time his pitch was over, we had signed the bottom line, and while we were a bit uneasy about the whole thing, our excitement over a gargantuan set of encyclopedias giving us vistas into the world outweighed any anxiety. All we had to do was write a review of what we thought of the books once we had a chance to look them over. That was it—almost. The publisher produces an "*Annual*," which includes updated articles about the information in the encyclopedias. We were required to buy one—that's 1—*Annual* for the next 10 years.

After the excitement passed, something just wasn't sitting right with us. As a soldier making less than $400 a month, anything extra was a stretch. After thinking about the whole deal, I realized that the "free" set of encyclopedias would end up costing us close to 500 of 1970s dollars. Fortunately, the laws of the state we were living in allowed for a seventy-two-hour period of reconsideration. We canceled our "free" books. A life lesson learned.

The salesman didn't lie to us; he just didn't tell us the whole truth, at least not in a way that we understood clearly. Since those days, I have become keenly aware of how deceptive partial truth can be. It's a minor insult when someone is duped out of a few bucks; it's another to be duped into believing something that pierces one's soul. Anger with a passing salesman is vastly different than being angry with one's Creator.

Have you ever been angry with God? I have. Have you ever shouted at God? I have. Have you ever questioned God's goodness or protested His lack of action on your behalf? I have. Have you ever said out loud, "I just don't get you, God!"? You should have been a fly on the wall of my office a few days ago. I have read the Bible cover to cover most years since I gave my life to Jesus over thirty-five years ago as a young man in my early twenties. I have been blessed more than I ever have imagined, and yet I am still not exempt from the disillusionment and disappointment that nags when God—according to my puny view—fails to intervene in my life or the lives of those I care about. I just want you to know up front that this pastor is "real."

As I write this, not an hour ago, I received word that a man I care about had a heart attack and is scheduled for open-heart surgery at a hospital 150 miles away. A very dear friend of mine and my wife's is now in her third year of a brutal fight with a rare cancer for which there is no known cure. Two days ago, a brand new "brother" in the Lord was back in the hospital for the umpteenth time, despite many prayers on his behalf. I can recount many more such stories, but you have your own—I know; I've been a pastor for over two decades.

We all look for hope; even pastors crave a good word that will lift our souls above the anxiety of life on a planet that is broken. We scan the television, we may seek counsel through social networking, or we grab a book that promises something better. And then there it is, like a gentle breeze that cools the brow of the discouraged with momentary relief from the headache of the day. You log on to your Twitter account and you read:

"You may be in a difficult season right now, but God is breathing new life into your spirit. Your victory is already on the way."[1] This is an actual "tweet" from America's most popular pastor of positivity.

His words promise "victory." He tells me God not only knows what is going on in my life but that He has already begun to ease my pain, my worry, and my despair. It's just what I wanted to hear. I feel better already...but is it true? My car is being repossessed, I am still unemployed, and nothing changes—or even gets worse. You pray, and it seems your prayers bounce off the ceiling and the heavens are made of brass.

"Your victory is already on the way."

Try and tell that to the mom and dad standing in the rain at the grave of their sixteen-year-old daughter killed on prom night a couple days earlier in a car accident. Convince the woman sitting in front of you who was the "play toy" of her father, her brothers, her grandfather, and even a few neighbors from before she could talk until she left the prison of abuse, latching onto the first man to pay her attention.

"Your victory is already on the way." Well, where is it?

The "prosperity gospel," as it is called today, promises heaven of earth, presenting a god who exists to jump to your side whenever you call, granting whatever whim, wish, desire, or goal happens to be on your list at the moment. The only thing that matters to the prosperity god is that you are happy—however you define happiness—and he cannot do enough for you to see that come about. The so-called "good news" of the prosperity gospel is simply that the reason you are alive is to be happy, healthy, and materially engorged with all this world has to offer.

I cannot deny that it is an appealing message because it fits perfectly with the view *du jour* of who today's god is. It used to be that this god—purposely spelled with a small "g"—was the preferred deity of the masses, whether religious or not. Today, it is engulfing even those who see themselves as members of mainstream Christianity.

So who is the god you worship? Is He the mysterious, sometimes silent, sometimes gentle, sometimes hard God of the Scriptures? Is He the God of the Bible Who cares so much for you that He will, if necessary, hurt you in order to help you? Or is he the god of a syrupy love who abandoned his holiness with the passing centuries, affirming, applauding, or even accommodating man's sinful choices? Whatever your dream, whatever your want, your wish is his command. So who is the God of heaven? What can we expect from the God Who became flesh and lived in our place, and where is the balance?

The balance is found in getting reacquainted with the God of the Bible and His wonderful but sometimes hard truth of what we can expect while living in a world that is ravaged by the effects of sin.

The God of the Scriptures *is* a God of *love*. He is also a God of character, with a nature that is unsullied by human sentiment, and is not able to be manipulated by our protests when He acts contrary to our desires or when He seems to fail to act at all.

> The proper pursuit of a biblical prosperity begins with understanding that at the core of the counterfeit is misinformation, improper use of God's promises, and a manipulated use of God's revealed truths.

The reason it is gaining so much headway in the church of Jesus Christ here and abroad is because it is what people want to hear. But true love is not demonstrated in telling people what they want to hear. True love demands "speaking the [*whole*] truth in love …" and that means delivering the whole truth, even if the whole truth is disquieting (Ephesians 4:15).

In the most obvious examples, the God of the Bible is being represented as a vending machine. You merely insert your token of faith, press the button of your desired "blessing," and out it comes.

Perhaps you think that the prosperity gospel has not come your way, that it doesn't pertain to your faith journey. Are you willing to take a little self-examination? Answer these, if you are brave enough: Do you believe the Bible—the whole Bible—is truly God's Word? If you answer yes, then who and what has been the greatest influence on your faith journey, has it been the Bible? Have you ever read the entire Bible? Are you encouraged where you worship to read the whole Bible for yourself? Does your pastor preach the scriptures in context as they appear in the Bible, or does he talk about subjects or ideas and then sprinkle some verses on them here and there? Does your pastor ever talk about the harder aspects of God's nature and character? Does he ever tackle the more controversial aspects of the Bible, like the book of Job; the slaughter of men, women, and children in the Old Testament; or the meaning of Romans 1 and what it means that God gave men up to depraved minds? Has he ever expounded on the brutality and gore of the sacrificial system and why the blood and the gore were necessary?

One of the hallmarks of prosperity preaching is that it focuses on the shinier parts of Scripture while selectively ignoring the not-so-lustrous ones. The prosperity preacher emphasizes the great promises of God while ignoring just when, where, and how those promises will be realized. If, as a matter of habit, you derive your understanding solely from reading books *about* the Bible rather than by actually reading and studying the Bible, then you are vulnerable to the half truths of the prosperity gospel. It is the increasing nature of "Christianity" today.

In this book, I have endeavored to bring balance to the popular god of many of today's Christians with the God of the Bible who *is* loving beyond comprehension—but is not without rules. He *does* want to bless us but not in the midst of sin. He *has* given us many promises of joy and contentment, but many of those promises will not be realized in this lifetime but the next. And finally, there *is* victory assured to those who truly love the Lord, but that too is for a day when God rules and reigns and every knee bows and all tongues confess that Jesus Christ is Lord.

This is not just a book of hypotheticals or tiresome arguments. I have purposely illustrated the principles I write about with real-life examples punctuating the reality of the good and loving nature of God and His intimate care of those He loves—and those who love Him. With few exceptions, the examples come straight from my own life, and they are compelling, as you will see. I also use examples of the problems with the prosperity gospel by quoting numerous prosperity preachers and teachers in the marketplace today.

Finally, I explain that there is a genuine prosperity that comes from following the God of the Bible, but it must be pursued according to the counsel of God's wisdom for life, not merely for our own selfish gratification.

> At the end of the day, God's people must be drawn back to the singular fact that God created us for Himself and not the other way around. We must never lose sight of that.

1

PROSPERITY PASSION
IN PERSPECTIVE

> God, after He spoke long ago to the fathers in the
> prophets in many portions and in many ways, in
> these last days has spoken to us in His Son...For
> this reason we must pay much closer attention to
> what we have heard, so that we do not drift away
> from it.
>
> Hebrews 1:1–2a; 2:1

The travesty of the prosperity gospel is that it dares to
diminish Jesus, the One of whom the Bible says should
have "first place in everything." His prominence is by virtue of who Jesus is, not by virtue of what He can do for
us. The prosperity gospel, which encourages a demand
for God's gifts at the expense of a passion for the gift
Giver, misses the mark, to say the least.

Timothy Keller notes that the miracles Jesus worked
were not the sum of why He came or even why He
worked such miracles. Rather, he notes, "Jesus's miracles
are not just a challenge to our minds, but a promise to
our hearts that the *world we all want is coming*"[2] (emphasis mine).

Miracles are inspiring, and miracles may be admired, but the Miracle Worker is to be worshiped. Miracles, favors, and divine trinkets will pass away, but the Miracle Worker lives forever. And the Bible tells us He is coming again to bring the unsullied prosperity of "Thy kingdom come." That time is not here, not now; it is in the future.

The god of the prosperity gospel is not a god to be worshiped. He is a god whose spine is flaccid and whose character is capricious, and his preachers spout tidbits of truth sprinkled on top of prosperity anecdotes, leading many down a hard path of discouragement and despair, for no one receives it all *now*. But with the fanfare of the testimonies and all the frenetic hype witnessed on screen or at a gathering of hopefuls, it is easy for the *normal* Christian to be discouraged. It seems all others are receiving their healing, their blessings, their fortune, their heaven on earth, so why aren't they? And they are lead to believe the problem is their faith.

Using spiritual rhetoric, the prosperity taskmasters wittingly or unwittingly indict those they charge with a weak and ineffective faith. Yet most people are sincerely in search of hope only to have their hopes dashed when their favor isn't received. Worse still, they meander off, disillusioned and defeated, believing they have given God a try. In the end, they might very well wind up inoculated to the truth and impervious to the real gospel, the good news of our great saving God.

Fourteenth-century writer Dante Alighieri seemingly gives prophetic utterance in *Paradiso*, capturing the problem of a steady diet of empty calories served up by more and more of today's preachers. He writes, "Such fables, shouted through the year from pulpits-some here, some there…so that the wretched sheep, in ignorance, return from pasture, having fed on wind."

This just might be the most lethal aspect of the prosperity message. Week after week, month after month, the poor in spirit and the hungry in heart are left starving at the trough of what amounts to Christianized junk food consisting of the equivalent of potato chips and cookies.

Dante's next line, again prophetic, betrays our age of victimization, refusing to allow the devotees of prosperity off the hook: "But to be blind to harm does not excuse them."[3]

I have tried to imagine how it is that the peddlers of a false gospel are able to sleep at night. Is it that the affirmation of naïve crowds or the consolation of accolades from a world system that admires even the illusion of success lulls them to sleep? Have the majority of prosperity preachers innocently strayed over time from a truth they once embraced, getting caught up in the sensation of their own press releases? Or is it that they willingly and knowingly lead people to a buffet of artery-coagulating cuisine that looks good and tastes good but are so enamored by their own lifestyle of leisure that they no longer see nor care that their sheep are malnourished?

I cannot possibly know what transpires in the hearts and minds of such individuals. But that cannot preclude some kind of assessment of the fruit and motives—which are publically evident—concerning the people propelling the movement.

At the end of the day, everyone answers to God alone, and because God is gracious, God chooses to save people, sometimes even by way of a flawed message. I have little doubt that along the way, some people have been redeemed through the ministries of the men and women who have so corrupted the beauty of the gospel of grace. But we must never interpret God's gracious mercies and His ability to work through all manner of error in bringing one of His own unto saving faith as God's tacit approval of the flaws. I have heard all manner of sin justified over the years when an unquestionably sinful story happened to have a happy ending. This begs the question: How do we explain the fact that, in spite of such warped proclamations, some people do, in fact, meet Jesus?

I will answer with an amusing but true anecdote I heard years ago from a theologian who was part of a think tank called the Australian Forum. He was relaying the story of a man with whom he had made acquaintance. He befriended him and spent much time with him, trying to get him to come to understand the magnificence of our glorious Lord. At every turn, he hit dead ends, at which point he simply decided just to be his friend. One day, his unsaved friend invited him to go with him to listen to someone who was going to be speaking about "religious things." The theologian was not familiar with the man they were going to hear but viewed it as another opportunity to speak with his friend about Jesus. The event came, and they both sat there, listening intently. The theologian was straining to find something redeeming in the man's talk but was dismayed by the abundance of words devoid of substance and truth. At the end of the talk, the men went their separate ways.

A couple weeks later, the theologian met up with his friend, who apparently had experienced a significant life change. The friend was excited to talk with him about his newfound faith in Christ. As the theologian listened, it was obvious that his friend had become born again. In the conversation, the theologian asked his friend what was it that finally convinced him of what he had been trying to explain to him for months. His friend said it was the night they went to hear the man referenced above.

Utterly dismayed, the theologian was trying to make sense of his friend's newfound faith coming as a result of what they both heard preached that night. Although it has been over three decades since I heard him tell the story, my recollection is clear, though not verbatim. Excuse the paraphrase, but it is very close to what he actually said.

His conclusion was as follows: "I tell you, as a studied theologian for decades, there was not one shred of gospel truth in what the man said that evening. How was it then that my friend came to Christ that night? The only way I can explain it [*referring to Balaam and his donkey; Numbers 22:28*] is that God spoke through the mouth of an ass once in history, and he had done it again!"

Yes, "His ways are not our ways" and "The king's heart is like channels of water in the hand of the LORD; He turns it wherever He wishes" (Proverbs 21:1). Nevertheless, we must never take God's gracious sovereign plan in calling a person to Himself, using it as an excuse for all manner of quasi-Christian shenanigans.

2

GODLY PROSPERITY NEVER ECLIPSES THE GLORY OF JESUS

It is easy to be critical. Every pastor knows that. Even in the best ministries, there are always well-intentioned individuals who believe it is their gift to complain and point out every flaw of everything that does or does not happen. I deem such criticisms a result of what I call the "view from the cheap seats." Walk a mile in *my* shoes. There are also those, however, who, in great humility and with reserve, say relatively little, but when they do, you are hearing the voice of God. Such are the voices that honorable people of faith crave.

It is natural to single out flaws in others. It is not as natural to suggest solutions. And while I was reluctant to include as many autobiographical vignettes as I have, they serve to reveal the real practicality of the sometimes heady theological points made along the way. They also serve to portray a balanced perspective to the so-called "life more abundant."

There is *real* prosperity and well-being in the counsel of God's Word, but it bears little resemblance to what is being sold by more and more preachers and teachers across the globe. Yes, it is an international phenomenon.

My wife and I have traveled far and wide. I drive a Mini Cooper S and am an avid golfer. I enjoy a great restaurant, appreciate nice fashion. We have lived and are living a life of prosperity. But there is a proper pursuit of that prosperity that comes, not as the result of using God as if he exists for our purposes, but which comes as the by-product of faithfully giving up the right to one's life.

> He who has found his life will lose it, and he who has lost his life for My sake will find it.
>
> Matthew 10:39

Godly prosperity is the ironic fulfillment of one's life and often dreams, even as those dreams are laid before the precious Lamb of God. Paul capsulized such perspective confronted by the living Lord on that road to Damascus.

> I count all things to be loss in view of the surpassing value of knowing Christ Jesus my Lord, for whom I have suffered the loss of all things, and count them but rubbish so that I may gain Christ…
>
> Philippians 3:8

The fact is, God is pleased to "fully support those whose hearts are completely His" (2 Chronicles 16:9).

There is blessing and promise associated with faithful giving and service to the Lord. This is beyond dispute. But this must never be confused with the good news of God's reclamation of our lives. While there are the well-known preachers and teachers who tend to garner the attention, the problem is much bigger than just those who exhibit the most extreme examples of confusing the good news. Consequently, pervasive intrusion of the prosperity gospel into the mainstream of evangelical Christianity is a deep concern for the future health of the church.

Even in what are typically Bible-believing ministries and denominations, the men and women one sees on television and who write the books are inadvertently, by virtue of their success and popularity, compelling otherwise astute men and women to dilute the whole counsel of God's Word found in His Bible. In a quest to be upbeat and positive, there is an undeniable drift toward fanciful teaching. Much of today's biblical exposition is quite selective, out of context, and misleading, if not patently false.

Without doubt, there is a cost involved with respect to one's fidelity to the "faith once for all delivered to the saints." Jesus wasn't speaking to the air when He warned that, as time goes on, there will be increasing hostility to the truth of His teachings and the truth of who He is. At the same time, there seems to be an increasing reluctance to endure the cost. Some of this reluctance spawns from the message of the prosperity preachers who avoid any allusion to the more sobering realities of the walk of faith.

At our church in Maine, we have grown from a small fellowship of thirty-seven people to a church of over a thousand. This doesn't exactly put us in the class of mega church, but in our city of sixteen thousand people (metro Waterville is about thirty thousand), this is a remarkable pattern of growth. Yet in the past couple years, it seems we have plateaued and are, in fact, even losing some ground.

As I have repeatedly examined our situation, trying to figure out what we might be doing wrong or differently, the only pattern I see is that our rigorous stand on the teaching (and application) of the whole counsel of God's Word is costing us. We are passionate about the extreme love of God demonstrated to us daily, and His love is clearly our focus. But we do not ignore that He is also *holy* and still hates sin and that we live in a broken world that does not operate according to the rules of perfection, justice, and compassion.

For twenty years, I have taught the Bible one book at a time—the good, the bad, and the ugly. My assessment is that, as a church trying to reach our increasingly wayward culture, we are paying a price for refusing to soft-peddle the issues of our day. In the face of an increasingly hostile environment, we continue taking seriously the way that Scripture deals with the everyday realities of life on a sin-tainted planet. There is no way around it; the Bible, if preached with faithfulness, is culturally offensive. This world is not our home. If we lose sight of that, it becomes easy—if not natural—to accommodate the many urges trying to mold the church into something less offensive. When that is allowed, the gospel, the good news, of what God has done on His own initiative to restore our friendship with Him becomes confused. If that singular issue is confused, everything else also becomes confused—even the nature of God Himself. If today's "Christians" are taught to expect a "vending machine god" who exists for their pleasures, they will also expect a "vending machine church." As soon as the church does not deliver the right ministry, the right music, the right atmosphere, the right—you fill in the blank—they are off to the next church that will meet their demands. Designer faith is just one more extension of the prosperity gospel.

The issue of confused gospel truth is as old as the beginnings of the Christian faith. It is an issue the Apostle Paul alludes to in warning against various iterations of other belief systems that were co-opting the term *gospel*, even in his day. He was clear that they were distortions at best and counterfeits at worst. His language was not accommodating when he stated with emotion, "I wish that those who are troubling you would even mutilate themselves" (Galatians 5:12). The issue at hand was a dispute over the Jewish rite of circumcision and the resultant confusing of God's grace in accepting both Jew and Gentile apart from such rituals. Some people's insistence that circumcision was a mandatory requirement for everyone was putting a barrier in front of those of a non-Jewish heritage. Paul was not about to allow such a hindrance to the message of grace go unchallenged. The likelihood of the good news getting obscured was more than he could tolerate. The intensity of his language reflects the importance of what was at stake. Our translations are somewhat sanitized from what Paul actually expressed. The word we read, *mutilate,* refers to castration in the original text. Paul was passionate, not perfect . . .

As the prosperity gospel grows in acceptance, the magnificence of the work of Christ is getting buried beneath a culturally selective and self-centered message that is misleading the masses with increasing regularity. This must not go unchallenged. Men and women desperately seeking the meaning of their lives, looking for hope and truth deserve better; more importantly, Jesus, Savior and Lord, deserves better.

3

A PERSPECTIVE
ON PROSPERITY

Something is glaringly obscene with the messages that pervade much of what is broadcast through the medium of television, best-selling books, and some churches that are larger than many of the towns in my part of the world called New England.

> If the popular notion of prosperity, health, and wealth is true, it must be true without respect to geographical location, historical epoch, type of government, or country's GDP.

Sometimes one has to remove themselves from familiar environs to see clearly.

It was March in my home state of Maine, and I was seated in what our team called the "flying tube." We were headed ultimately for the island of Hispaniola. Leaving from south Florida, we were headed for Provo, a beautiful little island punctuating the serenity of an otherwise endless emerald sheet of Caribbean water. Before I ever arrived at Faith Evangelical Free Church as pastor, the small body of people from Waterville, Maine, had been involved with an indigenous Haitian pastor in his village of Terrier Rouge.

Our magic carpet was a long, thin fuselage with one row of seats on either side of the propeller-powered aircraft and barely enough headroom for me to clear my five-foot-seven-inch frame. We had been in the air a few hours and needed to make a brief stop to refuel before our destination of Cap Haitien. After some time in the air, our pilot, who was essentially part of our seating arrangement, given the tight quarters, yelled over his shoulder, asking if anyone wanted some lunch. I thought he was joking, but he leaned over and took the top off a small chest cooler beside his seat and started handing little plastic boxes called Oscar Mayer Lunchables over his shoulder one by one while we passed each unit back to the person behind us until everyone was served. Few of us drank the soda that came later. There was no toilet on board.

We made our approach into Cap Haitien, a city on the northwest side of the island where Columbus landed prior to "discovering" America. I had no idea what I was in store for upon stepping off the plane. I left wintertime in Maine the day before but now was dealing with the searing Haitian heat intensified by its reflection off the tarmac of this crude airport. My first indelible impression of this poverty-stricken country was the smell that was heavy of burnt and burning rottenness. I have no touch point in my vast life experiences from which to draw for describing the stench further except to say it was a putrid, hanging denseness that was a little bitter in my mouth.

As we stepped through the gate, we were nearly mauled by locals wanting to take our bags, for a tip of course, carrying them the thirty-foot distance to our drivers waiting in jeeps that looked questionable as to their travel-worthiness. We were warned not to surrender them, as more often than not, though the distance was short, you were not likely to see your bags again. We'd been on the ground for less than thirty minutes, and I already wanted to go home.

We jumped into our fully depreciated vehicles and began the trek to Terrier Rouge. We would meet up with our host, Pastor Apollon Noel, the man who oversees the church, the feeding program, the clinic, and school for the nine hundred-plus children who are fortunate enough to enter the school. The ministry also provided a lunch of rice and beans three days a week. We were a team of eight from our church on a short-term mission trip, though I wasn't at all certain why we were there. It seemed to me what the people of Terrier Rouge desperately needed was our money, not our man power.

It was mentally confusing that just one day earlier, we were driving through Boston on a super highway, observing the Leonard Zakim bridge that was a veritable work of art in progress, looking more like an artist's rendition of a futuristic harp than a bridge with a practical function. In a half hour or so, our jeeps were halted as the makeshift bridge of scraps spanning the twenty-foot stream we needed to cross had recently been washed away by unusually heavy rains. My mind and body were going through so many changes that I found it difficult to speak.

I remember just shaking my head, mumbling, "Unbelievable!"

At one point, I did manage to utter to a traveling partner that I felt like I just stepped into a National Geographic photo shoot that I remember seeing as a child flipping through the pages of those mysterious magazines.

Most people along the dusty, pot-holed, packed-mud thoroughfare were clad in anything they were able to find. For some, that was barely anything at all. Style was irrelevant, cut of clothing a nonissue. Color coordination was unknown, and fit or even gender-oriented considerations were not part of the, *what do I wear today?* thought that looms so large to those of us who know nothing of poverty. I always thought the poor were the people in line at the grocery store with overburdened grocery carts, paying for their bounty with food stamps.

Again, I had no categories for what I was seeing, smelling, and feeling as we made our way to the place we would be staying for a few days. The density of people lessened greatly the farther away from the city we drove. The dwellings of the city, though dilapidated and disheveled, were at least recognizable as buildings. Away from the city, the nicer homes would be a single-room shack constructed of scraps of anything salvaged from anything—and I mean anything—utilizable. The lesser shelters were made of sticks, with vegetation used as wallboard and roofing.

As we entered the village of Terrier Rouge, people were roaming aimlessly with no discernible destination. Work is hardly a consideration, with the estimated number of unemployed between seventy and eighty percent.

I was overwhelmed and in a minor state of shock. The "healthy" looking people were sitting along the road, sometimes in little enclaves, sometimes around the vestiges of a fire pit of some kind from the night before. The not-so-healthy were lying along the side of the road, waiting to die, I supposed.

As we approached the residence of Pastoral Noel, the man we came to serve and the man with whom we would be staying, I saw another man who looked to be aged, but it was hard to tell with people so malnourished and with no medical care at all. He had a piece of cardboard big enough and worn enough to roll around him at night. That was his home, and I broke down and wept.

We're going home when? I wondered to myself.

Throughout the nine days we were on this "mission of mercy," just about each one in our group of a dozen— at least the first-timers—had their moment of wandering off to be alone and weeping.

We settled into our luxury accommodations with our Haitian host. Pastor Noel lives in a concrete block home with several rooms and even a shower when there's water. The cooking area is outside in back of the house, where meals are prepared on open fires. By Haitian standards, he lives extremely well. By our standards, his was closer to one of our homeless in this country fortunate enough to find a shelter each night.

The men stayed in one room, lying on floors or cots, attempting to go to sleep after church services, which were each night. There was no electricity per se, although a generator occasionally provided for bursts of power for special uses when they were lucky enough to find gas to purchase.

Nighttime was brutal. Lying in a room with other sweaty men with no air conditioning, no fans, and no air movement, you have to leave windows open to capture the rare but hoped-for zephyr of wind that might waft into the room. For the moment, the temperature might drop down to the mid-eighties, with a humidity to match, but with the windows open, you, of course, invite an invasion of pestilence. The mosquitoes invariably make their way through breaches in the shutters, bringing their incessant concert as the crescendo and decrescendo of whining wings is capable of driving one to near madness. The bloodthirsty, malaria-carrying pests conduct sortie after sortie of air strikes on your face and head. To combat the possibility of disease, little circular anti-mosquito coils are lit and left smoldering through the night in your room. I am one of those people who don't sleep well in climate-controlled, sound-controlled, pest-controlled luxury. And when you're allergic to smoke as I am, sleep deprivation is part and parcel of the whole short-term experience.

How many more days until we leave?

It was time for my first experience with the Haitian church. The darkness was so deep it was palpable as we strolled down the dirt road the quarter mile or so to the church building. We were engulfed by an amoebic swarm of children who loved the white missionaries who came to visit. Besides the novelty of blonde-haired, blue-eyed strangers, such visitors usually brought various treats of gum or candy with them. In fact, we purposely prepared for our trip, wearing clothing that we had planned on giving away or leaving behind for this people who had nothing.

As we walked in abject darkness, many little hands made their way into my pant pockets, exploring the depths (we were forewarned) for whatever they might find. I was remiss in not removing my watch before our ten-minute journey, and again, little hands were nearly successful in lifting it from my wrist. It was part game, part survival.

If the Prosperity Gospel Isn't True in Haiti, It Isn't True in America

The church was crowded with people of all ages, and the little children were all attentive and quiet. Amazing. Several people came up on stage, and the singing began without benefit of instruments, projection technology, sound systems, microphones, or amplification. The people were clapping joyfully as the Creole tongues of worship pierced the darkness.

As the preacher from the States and the sponsoring church of the mission, I was expected to address the congregation. But I had been struggling from the moment I arrived on the island as to what I might say. These Haitian Christians had a jubilant love of God in spite of living in a day-to-day routine of genuinely not knowing if they would even receive a single meal that day. When they prayed, "Give us this day our daily bread," it was a serious request, unlike our perfunctory ritual.

I was having sequential flashbacks of my frenetic ways in church back home as I fretted about everything from the temperature of the sanctuary to the quality of the video presentations. Would our drummer get his entrance right into the next song, and would the mix of the vocals be at the right levels for each part taken by our singers? Thinking of what I might say to these faith-filled believers, all I could imagine was, *I have nothing to say to these people. I have need of sitting in their presence and learning the reality of the sufficiency of God and what it means to be joyful in the Beloved, even when He doesn't jump through my hoops.* But I was "on." I stood next to the translator with all this going through my mind, and I forced something out, pretty much saying what was going on in my head.

> Back home we have so much more than what we need, and yet our joy of the Lord is more often contingent on His coming through for us in all the ways *we* have determined that He should. We talk about being captivated by His presence, but truth be told, we are more often than not infatuated with His blessings...

I was humbled and never felt so unworthy to address a group of people before or since.

Can I go home now?

As I thought of all the pleasures of life I had and yet how often I complain, I just didn't want to talk anymore, not as the preacher from America whose talk of faith was well beyond the reality of it.

Doesn't blessing follow obedience? I certainly believed it did, taught it did, and even experienced the axiom played out through thirty years of my own pilgrimage. Is the prosperity gospel really that distant from God's blessing of prosperity that follows obedience?

If entering a life-changing, life-saving relationship with the Living God is synonymous with material ful-

fillment, financial prosperity, familial peacefulness, economic advancement, and alleviation or avoidance of all
physical and emotional distress, how does one assess the
obvious disparity of people in Third World countries
who truly love the Lord? If the prosperity gospel is good
news, why isn't such good news realized in all parts of
the world, and why wasn't it realized during turbulent
times in history? Even in today's global community, love
for Christ might cost one his livelihood, his freedom, or
his life.

The Prosperity Gospel Is Offensive
to Persecuted People

That this life is hard is an obvious fact of our existence.
It is hard for the follower of Christ, and it is hard for
those still on a pilgrimage searching for truth. The history of the human race is punctuated by hardship and
struggle. There is just no way around that. For the follower of Christ, however, the difference is remarkable.
We are promised both: a better day in the future, as well
as a Friend to traverse the difficult roads we all travel
now. God said, "I will never leave you nor forsake you!"

Thank you, Jesus.

The truth is, those of us who have known little of
the world outside of the prosperous West have difficulty
coming to grips with the reality of the purpose of life.
Oftentimes, that is precisely because we have it so good.
But not everyone has had such charmed lives. Six million people in the land of China meet in secret places,
risk their lives appropriating Bibles, and face prison or

worse simply for loving Jesus. Try and sell them today's "prosperity gospel."

There are few people in modern times having the wisdom and life experience to pontificate on such a weighty issue as the purpose of life. Writing from the experience of the Soviet prison camps, Alexander Solzhenitsyn informs us succinctly and in the power of the spirit of God, "The meaning of earthly existence is not, as we have grown used to thinking in prosperity, but in the development of the soul."[4]

The hard truth is that a tendency of suffering in this life is more normal for the Christian than the promise of perfect health and extraordinary wealth. The statement might seem strained to those of us surrounded by opulence compared to the rest of the world. I suspect it is not nearly as implausible to a follower of Jesus living in less prosperous regions of the world or in a different epoch. I cannot imagine the faithful Jesus lovers of Auschwitz, Buchenwald, or Bergen-Belsen pondering a message of prosperity as typified by the sentiments of today's prosperity preachers.

Consider: The day before I finished writing this chapter, I received an e-mail from one of our folks working abroad in what is called a "closed country." The following is an excerpt from that e-mail.

> I wanted to bring you news of what has been going on over the last three weeks since I have written. Over 40 foreign believers (ex-pats) have been deported from the country over the past three weeks. This past week, [*the country's name omitted*] believers from our city and a few other prominent cities were arrested, interrogated, and

held in prison for several days. Several of them were beaten. [*Man's name omitted*], one of the men from our city, is the believer whose story I shared with many of you last spring while I was home in the States...he was held in prison for 4 days last week and badly beaten. He did not renounce his faith, which he is very glad about, and is trying to lay low for now. Another young woman from our city, a mother of two small children, was arrested, interrogated for several hours, and held overnight before she was able to rejoin her family. Please continue to lift up these friends, along with their families and the others who have been touched by this recent persecution.

In these days of so much gloom and doom, we need hope; we need to believe that there is a brighter day ahead. But is material wealth (here and now) an integral part of God's plan of redemption, with physical health (here and now) guaranteed in the resurrection of the Savior? Are the purveyors of prosperity merely guilty of overemphasis, or have their declarations obliterated the unsullied magnificence of the incarnation and its eternal significance to mankind? The reality of life in a fallen world begs the question: How does the so-called prosperity gospel fare when pressed through the sieve of God's Bible? What follows is an inquiry grounded on the inspired, infallible, inerrant, authoritative Word of God.

4

PILGRIMAGE TO A PROSPERITY PANORAMA

It is in difficult times that the religiously complacent and even the generally nonreligious are often awakened to one's mortality. When there is no one else to turn to and human ingenuity has played out its hand, one often turns to God, even as a last resort. This can be a time of great enlightenment, a time when, in our extremity, we are awakened to what is truly important in life and what a gift this life is. No wonder Jesus seems to give special consideration to those who are economically or socially disadvantaged. For those who are constantly awash with the blessings of material prosperity, it is easy to take the most important things in life for granted in exchange for a vigorous pursuit of earthly pleasures. Nevertheless, God, in His severe mercy, goes to extraordinary means to bring those He loves to His point of view. My life is a case in point.

The First Church of Christ Scientists in Arlington Heights, Illinois, would be the first church I stepped into since my early childhood. I was in high school, and it was of my own accord that I accompanied my parents to Sunday service. I had always known there was a God, and somehow, living in America, where the gospel is culturally pervasive, I knew about Jesus, if only vaguely. I knew that He was the Son of God—whatever that meant—and that He died for my sins. That I knew that much is ironic, for the teachings of Christian Science do not affirm either one of these tenets of orthodox belief, but that was something I would only learn later on.

In true American fashion, our family claimed a benign Protestantism, and with chronic family relocations, church attendance fell by the wayside. Spiritual pilgrimages sometimes take one down winding paths to destinations only later appreciated. I had no idea then that my wandering in the desert of Christian Science would yield insight into the mirage of the prosperity gospel decades later. Still, I had a faith of my own, and while it was infantile, it stood rock solid as God revealed Himself to me through the beauty of His creation.

I loved being outdoors, and from my earliest memories, it was there that God's presence seemed palpable to me. In one of our hasty moves out of town and out of state, we did a stint in suburban St. Louis. A monastery was situated within walking distance of our townhome. As a youngster in the seventh grade, all I cared about was that it was quiet and beautifully situated in rolling meadows, with a large, fish-filled pond on its premises. Saturday mornings meant being up with the sun and snatching some bacon out of the refrigerator for bait as I headed for a morning with the Creator with my pole in hand. This pond was so infested with "sunnies" that there were signs posted telling young anglers to discard any fish they didn't want on the shore. Sometimes I had a friend with me, but as often, I was by myself, shooting line out of my ultra-light spin-casting reel, hooking bluegill after bluegill and chatting with God.

Talking with God as if He were sitting or standing next to me was perfectly natural. Years later, through the grid of God's revelation to mankind, I would come to learn that my experience was simply the unplanned, unlearned, natural response of one of God's creatures to His creatorship. The first time I read Paul's introductory words to the church at Rome, this part of my pilgrimage made perfect sense.

> For since the creation of the world His invisible attributes, His eternal power and divine nature, have been clearly seen, being understood through what has been made...
>
> Romans 1:20

God was invisible, but the proof of His existence was more certain to this theologically innocent preteen than even the wondrous world of His I was enjoying.

So we were a typical Midwestern family preoccupied with the busyness of life with no time for God in any organized way until tragedy descended on our household. Out of nowhere, my fifteen-year-old brother began complaining of headaches, and within a few short weeks, he underwent brain surgery for a deep-seated malignancy. I would never see him again. I remember talk of him doing well in recovery, but, as it was told to me, some valve in his head let go late one night a couple days after the surgery, and he never awoke. It was the first time I ever saw my father cry. I was twelve. It was an awful time for our family, yet God used it to open our hearts and minds to the inevitability of our mortality.

Adversity has a way of kneading the stone-cold heart into something malleable when the hands of a loving Creator are allowed to embrace it. It is unfortunate that we tend to measure the warm intimacy of God in our lives by some superficial standard of happiness. It really is a faulty ruler, and when it is allowed to be *the* measure of God's compassion, the Gospel of Jesus is easily replaced with the gospel of prosperity. If worldly happiness was our yardstick, we would have turned our backs on the Supreme Being and walked away. But sometimes when pain is deep and joy elusive, our spiritual sensitivities are their sharpest. God, in His compassion, will allow us to anguish for the moment if it means saving us from an eternity of sorrow. In the grand scheme of things, what we experience in this life is but the blink of an eye. God knows this well and is willing to allow those He loves to suffer if it will result in their catching the hope of His promises. The Apostle Paul understood this firsthand writing: "For I consider that the sufferings of this present time are not worthy to be compared with the glory that is to be revealed to us" (Romans 8:18). Still, the mystery of free will is that some respond to extremity by seeking more diligently for God, while others throw their hands up in disgust, bolting at the first mention of the Divine.

This is why throughout the history of mankind, instead of drawing closer to God in times of prosperity, man tends toward peril. Unfortunately, living in a nation of material "blessing," the realization of instant prosperity illustrates the allure of what seems like America's favorite rainbow. It holds the promise, or at least the illusion of a promise, of heaven on earth. Yet over and over again, the prosperity found at the end of that rainbow ends not in a pot of gold but in a latrine of despair. The disappointment realized by the unwitting victims of the prosperity gospel resembles the disappointment discovered by the victims of earthly prosperity. The magnificent hopes of America's lottery winners and their joys are grounded in the "blessing" of material prosperity. Yet a casual stroll through some of the biographical sketches of winners reveals how common it is that prosperity precedes tragedy.

> Gerald Muswagon was all smiles as his troubled life took a fairy-tale turn when he won a $10-million lottery jackpot (Canada). Within seven years, he had spent essentially all his winnings and in a state of depression he hanged himself in his parents' garage. It was called "a shocking end for a man who appeared to have the world at his fingertips, yet clearly never could grasp the instant fame and fortune he was handed through his lucky $2 Super 7 ticket.[5]

> Billie Bob Harrell Jr. had a common tale. His was a tough life, but he endured through and persevered, looking for a brighter day. One June day, he found it winning the Texas Lotto and a cool $31 million. But 20 months after winning, he took his life. According to the Houston Press, "an intra-family war looms over the remnants of the fortune, which may not even be enough to pay estate taxes. Shortly before his death, Harrell confided to a financial adviser: 'Winning the lottery is the worst thing that ever happened to me.'"[6]

As I write this, the national news is reporting that a Florida man has been missing—a man who, in 2006, won $30 million in the Florida lottery. Abraham Shakespeare's good fortune might have cost him his life.

> According to Fox News: "Shakespeare vanished months ago." Shakespeare, 43, won the big jackpot after buying a lottery ticket at a convenience store in a town called Frostproof, claiming later that he gave the last $3 in his pocket to a homeless man just before the winning numbers were announced. He talked about starting a foundation for the poor and insisted the money wouldn't change him. 'I'm not a material person,' he said in 2007. 'I don't let material things run me. I'm on a tight budget.'
>
> The money quickly caused him problems. A former co-worker sued him in 2007, accusing Shakespeare of stealing the winning ticket from him. Six months later, a jury ruled the ticket was Shakespeare's. Then there were the people constantly asking him for a piece of his fortune. 'They didn't wait. They just came right after they found out he won this money,' his mother, Elizabeth Walker, said recently."[7]

The ruined lives of noted lottery winners are obviously only one dimensional. But when the traits of an improper pursuit of prosperity become fused with our faith, the repercussions are more reaching. The improper pursuit of prosperity has been ruining not just individuals but entire civilizations since the origins of man. The prosperity of the community of Babel in the book of Genesis invited a special visitation of God—the kind of visitation no one wants. Using the literary device of anthropomorphism (giving human qualities to God for the purpose of explaining an historical event), Genesis records: "The LORD came down to see the city and the tower which the sons of men had built" (Genesis 11:5).

After settling in the land of Shinar, the people of Babel grew as a culture and as an economy. Life was good, the land plentiful. With their combined talents, intellect, creative genius, and prosperity, they built a tower of such unprecedented magnificence that even they were impressed. But the problem at Babel was that God had given mankind its marching orders (four different times in the first nine chapters), and those orders were to scatter over the face of the earth, dwelling in the good land God had given them.

What is telling is that with their newfound prosperity and talent pool, God was no longer a necessary consideration. They said, "Come, let *us* build for *ourselves* a city, and a tower whose top will reach into heaven, and let *us* make for *ourselves* a name, otherwise *we* will be scattered abroad over the face of the whole earth" (Genesis 11:4, emphasis mine).

With God out of the picture, God's purposes for them—to scatter and multiply—became subordinate to their purposes. The only thing that mattered to them was whatever their heart's desire happened to be. In this case, they decided *they* would make a name for themselves instead of letting *God* make one for them—a name that would be glorious and eternal.

> The LORD said, "Behold, they are one people, and they all have the same language. And this is what they began to do, and now nothing which they purpose to do will be impossible for them."
>
> Genesis 11:6

We tend to believe that the solution to most of our problems and the source of most of our happiness is found in making our dreams come true. And so to that end, we strive with heart and soul, pursuing the prosperity we believe will satisfy the longings of our being. But as we gain perspective from God's Word, it broadens our view of the prosperity panorama, helping us to see how devastating the allure of an improper pursuit of prosperity really is.

Many years ago, on one of our many family trips to see my wife's grandparents in Ocala, Florida, our visit coincided with the opening of Walt Disney's EPCOT Center. EPCOT is an acronym for Experimental Prototype Community of Tomorrow. As we explored Disney's vision of a futuristic community, the late Walter Disney—a committed humanist—made certain the humanist message was unmistakable. The apex of humanism asserts that there is no need for God, that man possessed all the ingenuity, curiosity, ability, and prosperity necessary to make the world better than it is. Through man's ability alone, climate could be conquered by enclosing cities, the oceans harvested as efficiently as farm lands, the geothermal resources of the earth utilized with inexhaustible abundance, and mankind could live in consummate peace. In fact, one of the messages piped into our ears as we were riding through one of the exhibits was, "Given enough time, man can [*and will*] solve anything." Interestingly, the words of Disney eerily echo God's indictment against the citizens of Babel: "Nothing which they purpose to do will be impossible for them."

It is never beneficial to abandon the Creator, and times of prosperity, rather than times of hardship, seem to inevitably foster a hubris that leads to leaving God behind. So Babel was in danger of utterly forsaking one of God's creation orders to multiply and fill the earth. True to the fulfillment of His sovereign will, as well as His respect for free will, God confused what had been a single unified tongue among all the inhabitants of Babel, compelling them to scatter over the earth, aggregating according to their new bond of common languages.

> "Come, let Us go down and there confuse their language, so that they will not understand one another's speech." So the LORD scattered them abroad from there over the face of the whole earth; and they stopped building the city. Therefore its name was called Babel, because there the LORD confused the language of the whole earth; and from there the LORD scattered them abroad over the face of the whole earth.
>
> Genesis 11:7–9

As a result of God's generous sovereignty, both His creation order remained intact, and the people retained their freedom of choice.

This pattern of prosperity chiseling away at one's dependence on and love for God has shown itself to be an historical regularity. It is not coincidental that many people who imagine their life's dream of getting everything they want suddenly get everything they want and are miserable or worse.

In the play *Lady Windermere's Fan*, Irish playwright Oscar Wilde empowers his character named Mr. Dumby to utter the profound remark, "In this world there are only two tragedies. One is not getting what one wants, and the other is getting it."[8] Mr. Wilde, himself an atheist, was able to grasp what so many God-fearers today seem to ignore. But as one peruses the pages of Scripture, it is evident that the norm for the people of the Bible was hardly comparable to what we see today in prosperous North America. The popular and increasingly ubiquitous message of health and wealth are antithetical to the wise counsel of God.

The truth is, tragedy can be a holy time. Clive Staples Lewis wrote, "God whispers to us in our pleasures, speaks in our consciences, but shouts in our pains. It is his megaphone to rouse a deaf world."[9]

This was the hard but tender lesson I witnessed when my brother died. But it can also be a desperate time when one might be inclined to take hold of anything that seems to offer a ray of hope, a sliver of comfort, even if it is little better than grasping at wind. It was my brother's death that compelled our return to the Church of Christian Science. It was an uninformed, even if sincere, attempt to lasso the love of God, but God cannot be separated from the truth of Who He is. So even in my misguided meanderings into Christian Science, turn-of-the-century poet Francis Thomson's "Hound of Heaven" was baying at my heels as I entered military service.

5

TRUE PROSPERITY BEGINS WITH THE TRANSCENDENT

The conflict in Southeast Asia was winding down, and as I graduated from high school, there was talk of abolishing the selective service system. But in 1972, Congress was still calling up young men for the draft. I was bored with the community-college/living-at-home scene while my friends and my girl were away at school. Hearing that those with a draft number under a hundred would be called up the next fall (my number was in the seventies), I decided to enlist and have a choice in what my training would consist of and where I would be stationed. Those drafted had no say in the matter.

After army basic, parachute training, and medical instruction (I was an infantry medic), all my training schools were completed, and I landed at Ft. Campbell, Kentucky, stationed with the 3/187th Infantry, 101st Airborne Division. Since everyone who enters the military must declare a faith affiliation and my only association to religion had been loosely Christian Science, I considered myself a Christian Scientist.

I was headed home one December for a Christmas leave with an engagement ring in my pocket. I was more than ready to pop the big question to my high school sweetheart. Sooner than later, I knew I would have to face my future father-in-law.

Fear of the unseen God is too easily relegated to a realm that is not real. When it came to my father-in-law-to-be, it was real; I was petrified of Ed Limp. Up front, he was everything I was not. Yet at our core, we were remarkably similar—something I would never dare suggest to his face. (Women really do tend to marry their fathers …)

I nervously entered the family room of his castle one evening, an intruder into the man's cave—or better, his lair. He sat on his couch with a newspaper engulfing his visage. I think I tried clearing my throat to let him know I was in the room, although I was certain he was aware of my presence, a reality he wished to ignore. I dared not speak his name. It took me more than ten years of marriage to gain the presence to utter it, and even then with great reluctance. Staring across the room at what looked like a newspaper with hands, I mustered enough nerve to push out, "I'd like to talk about our plans."

Ed didn't even lower the paper at that point, nor did he respond. I'm not sure who made the next move. I just wanted my intrusion to end, a desire that would be quickly realized. From behind his paper fortress of the *Chicago Tribune*, he grumbled, "I suppose you want to get married."

I tried sounding confident and mature, but my nerves betrayed me as I said, "Yes," with more air than voice.

With that, he vigorously folded the paper in half and, with obvious agitation, blurted, "You know how I feel about this," slapping the paper down on the coffee table while storming out of the room, leaving me there to stare at the walls. For the moment, it was a place of reverie. I was relieved that I was there alone.

Like many fathers-in-law-to-be, Ed was "unreasonable." After all, I had just turned nineteen, had one whole year of junior college under my belt, and was a private first class in a wartime army earning less than $400 a month. I would be short-circuiting Barbara's—his first-born child's—college career, taking her out of one of the best universities in the country to go with this generic Protestant (they were Catholic) to become a military wife, living in what I affectionately referred to as "Snake Navel," Tennessee. Admittedly, my father-in-law's consternation is something a man can only appreciate after having traveled several decades down the road of life, with dreams for his own daughters in tow. In hindsight, my father-in-law was reasonable, if not rather gracious.

Having served with distinction, my term of service came to an end in August of 1975. My new wife and I planned to move from Ft. Campbell to Tampa/St. Petersburg.

With aspirations of becoming a marine biologist, I had applied months earlier and was accepted to the University of South Florida in Tampa. My in-laws were thrilled, realizing I was actually carrying through with my stated intentions for a college education.

But in the intervening months of my last year of service, something life changing occurred. Two men in my squad of infantry medics who had been sloppy soldiers, druggies, and partiers had some kind of overnight change in their entire affect. Apparently they had "met Jesus," as the saying goes, and their lives were turned right-side up. As their squad leader, it was apparent to me that something profound had happened.

Somehow, in God's providence, they decided to target me as their *spiritual* project. For several weeks, they would bludgeon me with statements of criticism concerning the Christian Science religion. They would tell me that Christian Scientists believed this and that, to which I routinely protested, "But I don't believe that!" So I decided that it would be a good idea to find out what it is that Christian Science really teaches. I commenced reading the Christian Science manual, *Science and Health with Key to the Scriptures* by Mary Baker Eddy.

Although my own knowledge of the Bible was embryonic, I had been reading it with some consistency upon entering the army. When I came to page 23 of *Science and Health*, I read the following: "That God should vent his wrath on his own beloved son is divinely unnatural; such a theory is manmade."[10]

Mrs. Eddy was clear in her strange theology. Two pages later, she wrote, "The material blood of Jesus was no more efficacious to cleanse from sin when it was shed upon the 'accursed tree' than when it was flowing in his veins as he went daily about his Father's business."

Even in my relative ignorance of the Bible, I knew that Mrs. Eddy had just jettisoned the very foundation of the Christian faith. I continued reading the rest of her writings, which consisted of disjointed ramblings and a comprehensive redefining of words commonly used by Christians. Because of this etymological sleight of hand, on the surface, Christian Science seems Christian. In reality, it is a nonsensical system of doublespeak, new-speak (to use George Orwell's term), and utter confusion adhering to nothing even remotely biblical.

My rejection of Christian Science was immediate and complete. With a few months of personal instruction in the Bible by Frank and Gil, my two transformed barracks buddies, I was devouring the Bible in my free time.

One night on CQ duty (CQ stands for charge of quarters; when an NCO is required to stay up all night, manning the headquarters telephone and making routine checks of the barracks), I was reading a book by Hal Lindsey called *Satan Is Alive and Well on Planet Earth*. Somewhere into the book, there was a crude diagram of a cross with a scroll nailed to it—at least that is my memory of it. Lindsey explained what Jesus meant when He said, "It is finished."

The best way I can describe what happened next was that the God who I had known since childhood from afar was introduced to me up close and personal. Even as I write this, the tears flow as I reflect on that incredible night. I think I spoke out loud in the quiet of the early morning hours, thanking Jesus for making Himself known to me.

We make thousands of decisions in our lives which we may think have no bearing on anything other than the obvious immediate situation. And yet the eternal God whose ways are mysterious inserts Himself into our lives, shaping us and compelling us through the mundane and unspectacular rituals of our daily routine. My life changed that night. The true prosperity of God's peace and God's presence, personal and real, was sealed within my soul. Nothing this world has to offer comes close. When the Holy Spirit of God occupies the new believer, a life of transformation commences. The world is viewed differently, values begin to change, and life's passions begin to be transformed by the gentle work of God in His new creation. All too often, with great excitement, the new believer is not typically as gentle with those around them as the Lord is with the new believer.

Barbara was pregnant with our first child. Her anatomy and biochemistry were adjusting to a new life within, and her emotions were heightened by the mysterious play of hormones with the pregnant woman's physiology. I walked in one day after work and, with classic male brevity, informed her she was no longer number one in my life anymore. Ah, the wondrous sensitivity of a man…Feeling fat, unattractive, and very pregnant, she presumed I was telling her I had found someone else. She sprawled on our bed, weeping. Wisely, I intuited that further explanation might be helpful as I clarified that God was now the most important person in my life.

The next year was a time of inquiry and growth for the both of us. Bob, an acquaintance we had made in the course of our inquiry, was part of a para-church organization at Ft. Campbell called the "Navigators." The Navigators are active on college campuses and military bases primarily, but this particular group, which had been involved at Ft. Campbell, was going to be moving to Atlanta to establish a community ministry. Bob took me out to a restaurant one afternoon and talked with me about moving to Atlanta when my time in the service was completed. Barbara and I would have some older, more mature Christians to watch over us and help us grow out of our spiritual infancy, he explained. But more than that, he continued, we just needed someone to love us and care for us in our new life's journey where Christ was now Lord.

My poor in-laws. We didn't know this man except that we had been to his house once for a time of prayer and singing with some other soldiers whom the Navigators had also been gathering. Some of these other men and their wives were considering or already planning to move to Atlanta as well when they finished their term of service at Ft. Campbell. I told Barbara what Bob and I had talked about, and that quick, she was on board. It made perfect sense to us at the time. In hindsight, it seems utterly bizarre.

So when Barb told her folks that we and their first grandchild were not headed to Florida (where Barb's grandparent's lived) but that we were going to Atlanta with a group of people we hardly knew to be involved in some kind of ministry we knew little about, they were convinced we were trapped in some kind of cult.

My stock—which had nearly risen into positive territory in the eyes of my father-in-law, although barely—plummeted once again. Oh, what we put our dear parents through ...

6

PROSPERITY OF ANOTHER KIND

On our meager income, we established a home, I enrolled in the local community college, and Barbara and I were growing by leaps and bounds. We were, in fact, cared for by the people who moved to Atlanta from Ft. Campbell, all of whom had big hearts for Jesus.

There is something blissfully wonderful about two people exploring the Bible on their own. That is not to say that we do not need the help of wiser, more grounded people in our lives—quite the contrary. But too often, this pastor has seen too many people come up through the ranks of the church family with few convictions of their own. In other words, they have rarely, if ever, in any kind of consistent way delved into the Bible, allowing the Bible, with the aid of the Holy Spirit, to speak to their soul. It is far too easy to let someone else do the work of digging, studying, and questioning, allowing them to spoon-feed you well past the point of appropriateness. It is not a new phenomenon. The writer of the book of Hebrews laments, "For everyone who partakes only of milk is not accustomed to the word of righteousness, for he is an infant. But solid food is for the mature, who because of practice have their senses trained to discern good and evil" (Hebrews 5:13–14).

It seems the church today is bulging with "Christians" who are essentially clones of the many people who ever had input into their lives. As a pastor I am keenly aware that many people who have sat under my teaching of the Bible have adopted certain ideas and behaviors because they have confidence in my spiritual and personal integrity. In part, this is legitimate. Paul wrote to the Philippian believers, "The things you have learned and received and heard and seen in me, practice these things, and the God of peace will be with you" (Philippians 4:9). Adopting the admirable qualities, convictions, and habits of those whose lives are exemplary is part of maturing in the faith. But if that is the extent of one's inquiry, such faith will only ever be as sure-footed as the faith of those from whom the readers have "borrowed" the other person's convictions and faith. But like an infant, there comes a time when ingesting only the digestively simple will yield malnutrition and compromised health. And as the author of Hebrews notes, maturity is not just an increase of knowledge but a regimen of practice, applying the knowledge gleaned. That is when something learned truly becomes one's own.

My wife is a voracious reader. Her readings run far and wide, broaching all areas of literature. One day several years into our faith journey, she said to me with some anxiety, "I feel like I am a composite of everyone I've ever read, but I don't know what beliefs are my own."

When lion cubs are young, they stand by and watch their parents stalk, kill, and tear the flesh of their prey into bite-sized pieces for the cubs. They are being nourished physically *and* they are being educated practically. That phase of development doesn't last long. Soon, the cubs are stumbling as they participate in the stalking of their next meal, and in a short time, they are participating in the kill. Finally, they learn by example and by imitation (practice) to develop the skill of obtaining meat for themselves. The cubs that sit, contented to be fed only by others, will soon find that they will go hungry.

Every Christian is called to sink their teeth deep into the Word of God at whatever level of intellectual inquiry God has enabled them. As children of the Navigators ministry, Barbara and I were raised from the beginning to establish the spiritual disciplines of reading through the Bible annually, memorizing scripture, and praying to God as a matter of course. Only with a well-developed biblical grid established can a person filter the myriad voices proclaiming "truth." The tools for developing a biblical grid for life would be firmly established in us in our new home in the South.

With no savings to speak of and no place to live, we took all our worldly possessions, which were few, and found an apartment in Decatur, just outside of Atlanta. I enrolled immediately in Dekalb Community College, reasoning that I would get my second year of community college under my belt, as it was much cheaper than a four-year university. Our income consisted of living off the GI bill, going to school full-time, and working part time at Decatur Hospital as a nursing technician. Barbara and I determined that we would not put our little son into some kind of daycare setting. We believed that we were living according to God's priorities for life and that He had committed Himself to taking care of our needs.

> As far as we could tell from the pages of the Bible, the only prosperity God promised was giving us our daily bread, and even in that, we needed to exercise some responsibility.

So we budgeted our meager income in an elaborate system of envelopes and jars kept in a linen closet. They were labeled variously with "laundry," "groceries," "gas," "entertainment," and so on. When the cash in any given container was depleted, it was permissible to take from another, except one. The jar labeled "tithe" was untouchable.

Early on in our spiritual nurturing, while still at Ft. Campbell, Barbara and I attended a seminar sponsored by the Navigators. All I recall from the whole conference is a presenter talking about how to get out debt. Even though Barbara and I were not in debt, the phrase I remember from the man at this seminar of some thirty-five years ago is, "If you want to get out of debt, increase your giving."

While fears of cultic involvement were sounding even more ominous, his wasn't some manipulative ploy to get the conference attendants to give to the Navigators. His was a biblical instruction on the necessity of giving ten percent of your income (called tithing) to your local church as an act of thankful worship.

The notion of a tithe and the way it was spelled out in the scriptures seemed perfectly logical. Barbara and I were living within our means, so the idea of giving more to get out of debt was irrelevant. Nevertheless, the motivational aspect of the message—give with thankfulness and acknowledgement that God is Lord of everything, including our sacred finances—struck a chord. We started tithing from that day forward, through thick and thin, mostly *thin*, and what we have experienced firsthand is nothing short of miraculous. After many years of experience, I discovered that God's math is not found in the writings of Euclid or Pythagoras.

> Are not five sparrows sold for two cents? Yet not one of them is forgotten before God. Indeed, the very hairs of your head are all numbered. Do not fear; you are more valuable than many sparrows.
>
> Luke 12:6–7

That we have a big God who has His eye on the smallest of details in our lives was learned early on in our new life in Atlanta. To be sure, God's prosperity concerns providing our daily bread, but that does not mean He is unconcerned about the plate we put it on.

It's one thing to listen with wide-eyed wonder as Jesus talks about His concern for His feathered friends; it's another to make the jump to what's in my cupboard. Unpacking in our new apartment, we were short on drinking glasses—nothing special, certainly not something we couldn't live without—but Barb thought to herself we could sure use a few more glasses.

I don't know if she ever expressed that to the living God as an item for prayer, but within a day or two, a neighbor in our unit stopped by to introduce herself and welcome us to the building. She presented Barb with a package as a little house-warming gift. It was a six-pack of Libby drinking glasses.

Was Barb expecting in faith that a set of glasses miraculously appear like that? Hardly. Was there a pleading with the Maker of the universe to "release" what "should" be ours by right? Never. Instead, what we would discover in the ensuing years of our lives of faith is that God is delighted to give good things to His children. Why should that surprise us? He tells us as much:

> What man is there among you who, when his son asks for a loaf, will give him a stone? Or if he asks for a fish, he will not give him a snake, will he? If you then, being evil, know how to give good gifts to your children, how much more will your Father who is in heaven give what is good to those who ask Him!
>
> Matthew 7:9–11

Those glasses were one of the very least ways in which God showed Himself to us in practical ways over the years. But those glasses became an Ebenezer of sorts—something we would look back on over and over again, being reminded that this huge God of ours is concerned about the smallest aspect of our lives. We tend to expect a great God to step in when something immense in our lives is looming—something that is well beyond our ability. Somehow, though, we tend to think God just can't be bothered with everything else in life.

For the bulk of our time spent on earth, in the minutia of the daily grind, most Christians function as practical deists. That is, we believe in God; we might even believe many right things about God. But when it comes to the realities of living in a human world, God, we believe, is just too busy in other galaxies of the universe or is consumed by far more important needs on the other side of the world. So when the inconvenience of the clutch in our car stops clutching, we tend to think we're on our own. But why do we make such assumptions?

Our Datsun B-210 was a bona fide necessity of life. It had plenty of miles on it but many more to go. We were a one-car family, and it met our need for transportation. Best of all, it was paid for. I noticed the clutch slipping more and more, day by day until one afternoon, it just wouldn't allow me to shift gears. I managed to drop it at a place of repair, knowing roughly what it would cost. Technically, we had the money for the repair, meaning we could take the funds out of the envelopes and jars for other categories comprising our budget system, but, of course, that would leave us hanging in the all those areas from which we removed the funds. But the Datsun was an immediate, pressing need, and everything else could wait—everything except the tithe jar. Any thought of withholding our giving to the Lord's work never entered the picture.

> Look at the birds of the air, that they do not sow, nor reap nor gather into barns, and yet your heavenly Father feeds them. Are you not worth much more than they?
>
> Matthew 6:26

Yet again, a reference to God's care of birds. Could it be because we are bird brains when it comes to understanding some of the most elementary aspects of God's love?

I went to retrieve our repaired Datsun later in the day, was handed the key as I pulled out my checkbook.

"It's all taken care of," I was told.

I honestly don't remember my thoughts at the moment. But I know that I never had some perverse notion that I deserved such consideration being "a child of the King," as I hear some prosperity preachers insist. Instead, I both cheered in my spirit that this God is amazing yet equally wondered why I should receive such attention from this God who must be terribly busy. As I said, for much of our lives, we function as practical deists.

God's Prosperity Is Full of Wonder

Barbara was a full-time mom as I was busy with school and work and, in my spare time, raising my growing family. Another foundational aspect of life I learned early on in reading my Bible is that God expected me to be the leader of my home—not the brutish king of my castle, but the loving, gentle servant who was to exemplify the values of Jesus in all He taught and all He lived. Such a high calling in life is both wonderful and also wearing. Everyone grows tired. Even the Son of Man needed to get away from the demands of life, but in my mind, recreation was a luxury that was not going to be in the formula of our lives for many years. I have since learned that recreation, when properly viewed, is supposed to be re-creation; in other words, a time of rebuilding, of refreshment that prepares one to continue on in the service of the Lord, whatever venue in which that happens to take place. So actually, recreation is a bona fide need of the human condition.

I was driving in the car one week. The sun was brilliant, and it was one of those idyllic summer days. My mind was wandering, and I caught myself thinking,

Wouldn't it be fun to go waterskiing? Waterskiing? Where did that thought come from? I had only been waterskiing once in my life, and that was in high school when a girl-friend invited me to go with her family. *Waterskiing?* I thought. *What a strange thing to think of. Still, it would be fun...*

We had become acquainted with the neighbors next to us in our apartment complex. We didn't know them well but a little better than just saying hello before ducking into our cave, as was the cultural norm in suburban Chicago. This was the hospitable South, though. Out of the blue, a few days after my strange thought about waterskiing, my neighbor, Morris asked me if Barbara and I would like to come with him and his wife, Delia, to his "daddy's cottage," which was on a lake somewhere nearby. He said we would barbeque, do some waterski-ing, and just relax and have some fun. I could only shake my head in dazed disbelief. God's prospering us through the regular provision of our needs would be a hallmark of our faith pilgrimage through the years.

Another child came along not long after settling into to our new life in Atlanta. Health insurance was out of the question. We were not being presumptuous or irre-sponsible. If we could have afforded any insurance, we would have purchased it. But we were living paycheck to paycheck, and we lived by conviction that if we could not pay for something, we didn't need it. God promised He would take care of us if we were seeking first the kingdom of God and His righteousness (Matthew 6:33), which, to the best of our knowledge, we were.

Children were a blessing from His hand, and we trusted that if and when we became pregnant, God would take care of that as well. When our first child was delivered at Ft. Campbell Army Hospital, the only charge was for the food my wife ate during her brief stay. The total bill for our son was less than $11. Our new little girl, born in suburban Atlanta, was a bit more expensive.

I cannot recall how it was we managed to pay for our new gift, but we did and without payments. Being loved by God does not promise exemption from life's rough spells. Our children experienced the same childhood ailments as any other children. Ear infections were chronic and routine pediatric care; well baby visits, checkups, even antibiotics were somehow always resolved within our meager income. Like I wrote earlier, "God's math..." But the promises of God to prosper us do not exempt us from "the rain which falls on the just and unjust alike" (Matthew 5:45).

I graduated from Dekalb Community College and began the following year at Georgia State University, enrolling in the medical technology program. I had my sights set on medical school, which, in light of my dismal high school performance, was either delusional or was just additional evidence that when God takes control of person's life, nothing is impossible. As Paul writes to the believers at Corinth, "Therefore if anyone is in Christ, he is a new creature; the old things passed away; behold, new things have come" (2 Corinthians 5:17).

Matriculation at Georgia State University would be financially challenging; nothing new there. After making our calculations, adjusting our budget, it seemed that a best-case scenario would leave us $100 a month short from the start. Even in 1977 dollars, that was not an impossible amount, but it was substantial enough to give us pause but only for a moment. We were convinced we were doing what God wanted. We were honoring Him in all ways, and if He wanted this to happen, He would make it happen, and we wouldn't have to go in debt to do so. We would take it a step at a time and, if need be, could always bail and go to plan B, whatever that was.

Out of the blue, we received a letter from Barb's grandparents. Enclosed in their letter was a check for $100 with the note that they wanted to help us in our academic pursuit. The $100 would be a monthly gift until I graduated. Our need was taken care of and much more beyond that.

Barb's grandparents lived in Ocala, Florida, an eight-hour drive from Atlanta. Their home became our quarterly refuge when on hiatus for school break. Florida was a paradise of recreation, hanging back, loads of fun with my grandparents-in-law. Beyond the R and R, they would lavish us with replenishing our wardrobes and necessities of life as a young family. We were officially poor, yet we lived like affluent Americans experiencing profound prosperity.

Two years later, I received my B.S. in medical technology, working full time as a blood bank technologist at the Atlanta Veterans Medical Center. I was twenty-seven years old and decided to give medical school a try. I was not a great candidate for medical school from a grade-point consideration. While going through Georgia State, I could not afford to adopt the normal medical school mindset. Forsaking my family for the sake of a grade point was not an option. I was, according to God's priorities, first a husband, second a father, and third a student. Pursuit of my career could not ever supersede the wisdom of God in spelling out what was truly important in life. By this time, I had worked in the medical field long enough to see the toll that being a physician took on so many families. Most of the doctors I was familiar with were single, divorced, or essentially estranged from their families due to the consuming nature of the profession. It concerned me enough that I was ambivalent about my dream of being a doctor. Even at my adolescent level of faith, I realized that what I perceived to be my "best life now" was not necessarily His best life for me now. The salient consideration was, given God's priorities for me, could I be the kind of husband and father I knew God wanted me to be *and* a great physician facing another eight to ten years of schooling? Maybe God would drop me a letter spelling out His will for my life, but my skeptical nature probably wouldn't have accepted it, even if He did.

I am not a fan of what is sometimes known in Christian circles as "fleecing." The term comes from Gideon's desire for the reassurance of the Lord's promise concerning his upcoming battles. In Judges 6, Gideon is informed by the Angel of the Lord that He (God) was going to use him to deliver Israel from the Midianites. But when push came to shove, Gideon needed some extra reassurance that God would do what He said.

> Then Gideon said to God, "If You will deliver Israel through me, as You have spoken, behold, I will put a fleece of wool on the threshing floor. If there is dew on the fleece only, and it is dry on all the ground, then I will know that You will deliver Israel through me, as You have spoken." And it was so. When he arose early the next morning and squeezed the fleece, he drained the dew from the fleece, a bowl full of water. Then Gideon said to

God, "Do not let Your anger burn against me that I may speak once more; please let me make a test once more with the fleece, let it now be dry only on the fleece, and let there be dew on all the ground." God did so that night; for it was dry only on the fleece, and dew was on all the ground.

Judges 6:36–40

Desperate men do desperate things, and I prayed something along the lines of, "Lord, I don't know if you want me to be a physician or not. You know my heart's desire to be a doctor but, even more, a faithful husband and dad who is involved in my family's nurture. Most of all, I just want to be faithful to you always."

For those not familiar with the medical school protocol, the spaces for incoming students are relatively few, and the competition for those spaces is fierce. So it is routine to apply to numerous schools and is quite common to be rejected on first application. Reapplying the following year and even the year after is commonplace.

The second half of my prayer was the fleece. "I will apply to this one school only this one time, and if I don't get in, that will be the end of it." What I never anticipated was the possibility of another scenario presenting itself—one which could be seen as either God's will giving me what I hoped for or a temptation to pursue my own prosperity. When the time came to make that decision, He would make that clear.

Do not boast about tomorrow, for you do not know what a day may bring forth.

Proverbs 27:1

7

WHEN PROSPERITY AND REALITY COLLIDE

January 20, 1983, was unremarkable in the day of the world. It was a day of surprise—not the good kind—for my family. I had just picked my children up from a friend's house, where they were being babysat. They were three and five years old. I was taking them home, which was a mere two miles away. While I had developed the wise, not to mention safe, habit of never putting them in the front seat, much less strapping them in the same seat together, our house was practically around the corner.

I was a fanatical seatbelt user, but in our aging Datsun, only the driver's side belt receptacle worked in the front seats. There was one traffic light before home, and I was sitting at it, waiting to make a left-hand turn. We were less than a mile from our house. As I was waiting for the light to change, without thinking, I reached over and grabbed my children's seatbelt, pulled it across them, and clicked their belt into my receptacle. The last thing I remember to date is making the turn and glancing to my right to see children at play in a neighborhood park. Only seconds after making my turn onto the four-lane road, an intoxicated driver in the oncoming traffic lane had passed out at the wheel and slammed into our B-210 head-on.

Coincidentally, Barbara was also on her way home, being dropped off by a friend from church, and they chanced to pass the scene of the accident. Barb remarked to the friend driving that one of the cars looked like ours. They turned around and headed back toward the scene.

I awakened once in the ambulance, and then I don't remember anything until I was in radiology and the medical crew was cutting my pants off so they could better assess my injuries. By God's grace, my children survived, and by even more grace, I survived as well. Barely regaining consciousness, even then, my sense of humor was intact. I remember saying to the crew working on me, "This is the moment my mother always warned me about," explaining why I should change my underwear every day.

My head had taken out the windshield, my chest bent the steering wheel into a *V*, and my knees were broken and lacerated due to impact with the dashboard. My five-year-old son suffered a ruptured intestine from the seatbelt, and my three-year-old daughter received head and facial lacerations. Had they not been in their seatbelt, it is doubtful either one would have survived.

A friend from our church happened to be one of the police officers at the scene of the accident. The drunk driver, a habitual offender, in an all too common insult of the ironic, was arrested unharmed, laughing about what had just happened.

So where was God that afternoon? It is a common complaint in such dire situations of life. Didn't He know what was going to happen? Why didn't He stop the drunk from getting into his car or from taking that road at that time of day? Why did He allow me to deviate from what was an ingrained rule about children in the front seat, especially with only one functional seatbelt?

Such questions are understandable. At the core of our being—everyone's being—is a sense of eternity, of someone greater than one's self. Solomon wrote, in Ecclesiastes 3, that God has "set eternity" in everyone's heart. That includes the most hardened atheist, as well as the most devout believer. That gnawing sense of eternity is what produces the irritated accusation of the irreligious to any suggestion of there being a supreme being. When God doesn't respond to life situations according to what any individual determines to be "good," "compassionate," or "just," that person feels justified, indeed compelled, to indict any notion of an Almighty who is all-powerful yet perceived to be unkind and all-knowing yet slow to act, if at all. In such cases, it is easier to reject not just a particular perception of God but any idea of God at all.

Richard Nixon's cohort, G. Gordon Liddy, is an extreme example of the process some take in confronting the unknown.

As a frail child who was pretty much afraid of everything, Watergate conspirator G. Gordon Liddy tired quickly of his paranoia. His solution was to face his fears one by one, conquering them by facing them head-on, even if with psychotic resolve. To conquer his fear of lightning and thunder, as a child, he strapped himself up in a tree with a belt in the midst of a violent thunderstorm, shaking his fist in defiance. When he ran in fear from the rats on the wharfs of his hometown, he realized that rats were afraid of cats because the cats would eat them. So in Liddy's strange adolescent mind, it made perfect sense to capture a rat, roast it, and eat it, believing that the rats, of which he was petrified, would scurry at his presence knowing that he ate rats, just like the cats they feared. But Liddy's ultimate challenge came in confronting his fear of God.

Being raised in a strict Catholic school, he was punished if he failed to recite his evening ritual of prayer with precision. He was taught as a child that if he didn't say his bedtime prayers perfectly, he might not live to see the morning, as God would kill him. And since Liddy couldn't see God, capture Him, or eat Him, he chose to explain him away by an act of his will.[11]

Prosperity Isn't Always Fair

The very fact that within the heart of man there exists what philosophically is called "the problem of evil" is *prima facie* evidence that there is a God who is fair. If there is no God who is the authoritative embodiment of what is good and just, any idea of what is bad or unjust becomes nothing more than a construct. One person's idea of what is good might be the opposite of what another's idea of good might be. To one, it might seem unjust to enslave a person as another's servant, but to someone else, strength or power, class or education, color or—fill in the blank—might legitimize such oppression.

Indeed, without a Supreme Definer of good and bad, right and wrong, any suggestion of oppression is a *non sequitur*. Without a consummate *someone* who defines kindness either by fiat, by example, or both, there can be no unkindness. There can only be an existence where might is right, which means that what is right is determined by the one who, for the moment, has the might. Such a world would basically reduce *homo sapiens* to the same level as animals, where Darwin's notion of survival of the fittest would indeed be the supreme governing rule.

The world of the atheist is a world with untenable problems in all realms of life. In actuality, true atheists are in short supply, and atheism, which should not be confused with secularism, is not a significant driving force in culture.

> Far more devastating to the human spirit is not the world of the godless, but the world of the "godly," which, instead of explaining away every notion of God, has instead made Him in *their* image and likeness.

This is not the God of Scripture; this is the reinvented god of the prosperity gospel.

Perhaps nothing has had a greater impact in fostering such reinvention of God than the troubling situations of life where bad things happen to good people—that is, when God fails to act as we have determined He should. There is perhaps no greater formula for disappointment (at best) and a loss of faith (at worst) than evaluating life through the eyes of a false, even if popular, god.

In 1981, Rabbi Harold Kushner penned the bestselling book *When Bad Things Happen To Good People.* Kushner, beset by his own heartache at losing a child afflicted with progeria (a genetic disorder causing premature aging), set out to give answers as to why God permits such things. While I commiserate with his and his wife's loss, his answers were and are profoundly lacking. Kushner's solution is that while God is a kind and benevolent deity who means well, He is simply incapable of doing anything about the suffering in the world.[12]

Holocaust survivor Elie Wiesel says of Kushner's god, "If that's who God is, why doesn't he resign and let someone more competent take his place?"[13]

Some, like Liddy, reject any notion of God out of hand, perhaps the penultimate argument by assertion. Others, like Kushner, choose to adopt a grandfatherly type of god who has a good heart but is impotent. Other solutions to this confounding sense of an unfair world are dealt with variously.

Some choose to see a world that *is* fair—that is, that everything that takes place in the world *is* just, and anything that appears otherwise is met with a skeptical response. Common sense, however, must regard such a view as nonsense. This view of the world is errantly grounded in a causal system of utter fairness which asserts that one always gets what one deserves in spite of evidence to the contrary. One Psalm is particularly helpful in seeing that the world is not a place that is fair.

Prosperity of the Perverse Has Always Spawned Irritation

A man by the name of Asaph writes candidly, revealing that he too was annoyed by the apparent injustices in this world. But for Asaph, not only did the good seem to be punished, but those who behaved poorly were actually rewarded.

Psalm 73 deserves some scrutiny.

> Surely God is good to Israel, to those who are pure in heart!

Asaph begins well, declaring what he believes to be true—at least at a certain level. God is good to His people, and He is good to those whose hearts desire what He desires. Asaph has declared what is right. But he has a significant problem.

> But as for me, my feet came close to stumbling, my steps had almost slipped. For I was envious of the arrogant as I saw the prosperity of the wicked.
>
> Psalm 73:2–3

His issue is that what he believed to be true about God in his head was not born out in his experience of the daily grind with his feet. This was a significant enough "issue" that he was growing weak in his resolve to remain pure in heart, to desire what God desires.

Asaph explains, continuing in Psalm 73:

> For there are no pains in their death, and their body is fat. They are not in trouble as other men, nor are they plagued like mankind. Therefore pride is their necklace; the garment of violence covers them. Their eye bulges from fatness; the imaginations of their heart run riot. They mock and wickedly speak of oppression; they speak from on high. They have set their mouth against the heavens, and their tongue parades through the earth. Therefore

his people return to this place, and waters of abundance are drunk by them. They say, "How does God know? And is there knowledge with the Most High?" Behold, these are the wicked; and always at ease, they have increased in wealth.

Psalm 73:4–12

Asaph's take on life is pretty contemporary. Indeed, many aphorisms still in vogue today, such as "The rich get richer, and the poor get poorer," "No good deed goes unpunished," "Only the good die young," seem like they could have been written more than 2,500 years ago. Asaph's protest as to the unfairness of it all caused him to ask, "If this is true, what is the point of obeying God?"

> Surely in vain I have kept my heart pure and washed my hands in innocence; for I have been stricken all day long and chastened every morning. If I had said, "I will speak thus," behold, I would have betrayed the generation of Your children.
>
> Psalm 73:13–15

The underlying power of his protest is the assumption that good is rewarded and evil is punished, that life is laid out in such a way that justice is always immediately realized or pretty close to it. He is exasperated when he thinks of how many times he has done what is pleasing to God and yet winds up getting the short end of the stick. If obedience to the Living God doesn't pay, what's the use?

This is such a present-day problem. As a pastor for over two decades, I have the same thoughts more often than I would care to admit. And I know the answers.

Nevertheless, there is that interwoven sense of divine justice in our souls that causes us to crave fairness and recoil at unfairness, at least when we are the ones receiving or not receiving what we think we ought. But Asaph isn't done telling his story. This isn't the kind of doubt he voiced out loud. To do so would be to stumble the less informed, the less experienced, but he brings out the key to his success in trying to unravel the perverse and unfair way the world operates.

> When I pondered to understand this, it was troublesome in my sight until I came into the sanctuary of God; then I perceived their end.
>
> Psalm 73:16

What was the key to Asaph's coming to grips with the unfairness of life? It wasn't by squeezing the machinations of a fallen world through some man made grid that is short sighted and one-dimensional. If one is to assess all the goings-on in a world that is governed by less than perfect humans, you cannot expect a world of fairness. The breach that Adam and Eve ushered in by disobeying God in the garden did irreparable harm (for the time) to the entire scheme of life on planet Earth. And this breach will not be repaired until God comes again to repair the breach. So unfairness is not an abnormality but, in fact, is the norm.

When people were standing around Jesus, assessing the collapse of the tower of Siloam, where eighteen people were killed, their apparent assumption was that the ones who were killed must have had it coming to them. But Jesus chides them for their unfair assessment of the tragedy.

> Do you suppose that those eighteen on whom the tower in Siloam fell and killed them were worse culprits than all the men who live in Jerusalem? I tell you, no, but unless you repent, you will all likewise perish.
>
> Luke 13:4–5

Asaph illuminates us as he was illuminated, contemplating the unfairness of life not from an earthly vantage point but from a heavenly one. Speaking of the wicked, he says, "Surely You set them in slippery places; you cast them down to destruction. How they are destroyed in a moment! They are utterly swept away by sudden terrors! Like a dream when one awakes, O Lord, when aroused, You will despise their form" (Psalm 73:18–20).

It dawns on Asaph that this life does not guarantee justice, *but* there is a future day when every wrong will be righted and every right will be rewarded, as it should in a perfect universe. But now is not necessarily the time. We might and, in fact, do receive glimpses of justice through the systems of God's grace that he has instituted for our benefit (cf. Romans 13), but consummate justice and fairness is for a future day. And Asaph nearly misses God's view of life because of his seething at the way a corrupted world behaves. If left unchecked, it is enough to drive even a God-loving man or woman to places of rage with an outcome of craving vengeance *now*.

Asaph's travails serve to bring us beyond the circumstances of the immediate situation(s) to the invigorating and encouraging *Rock*, who never wavers, even as it carried him.

When my heart was embittered and I was pierced within, then I was senseless and ignorant; I was like a beast before You. Nevertheless I am continually with You; You have taken hold of my right hand. With Your counsel You will guide me, And afterward receive me to glory. Whom have I in heaven but You? And besides You, I desire nothing on earth. My flesh and my heart may fail, But God is the strength of my heart and my portion forever. For, behold, those who are far from You will perish; You have destroyed all those who are unfaithful to You. But as for me, the nearness of God is my good; I have made the Lord GOD my refuge, That I may tell of all Your works.

Psalm 73:21–28

This is a hard pill to swallow. We hate to wait. I hate to wait. I want to see God act in righteousness *now*, at least when it's convenient for me.

Deep Down, We Tend to Believe That a Lack of Prosperity Is Always Deserved

Remember the people of Jesus's day inquiring about the man born blind? Through some misfortune of birth, a baby came into the world without eyesight. And the people inquire about the blind man, now an adult, with their assumptions glaring.

And His disciples asked Him, "Rabbi, who sinned, this man or his parents, that he would be born blind?"

John 9:2

Apparently there was no room for random imperfection in these people's world. If a baby comes into the world with some kind of birth defect, in their view, it was necessarily indicative that either the parents had sinned or the man had sinned. In their view, there was such a causal relationship between behavior and "blessing" that any misfortune—even prenatal misfortune—must necessarily have been caused by someone's poor conduct. The prosperity preachers of today perpetuate this same view of the world every time they promise health and wealth, making it contingent on one's ability to "have faith."

Jesus must have rattled the preconceived ideas of the people of his day when he answered, "It was neither that this man sinned, nor his parents; *but* it was so that the works of God might be displayed in him" (John 9:3, emphasis mine).

Interestingly, the better one gets to know God, the more mysterious He becomes. Jesus's answer presents an additional challenge about the nature and character of God. The man came into the world blind, not simply with God's approval (His permissive will), but by God's design (His decretive will) precisely to the end that God could use the blind man, in God's timing, for God's purposes.

Such a suggestion should rock the prosperity peddlers on their heels. The suggestion tends to be an affront to our sensibilities when we entertain the thought that God might just permit something negative to happen that He could have prevented. Still, it is an altogether higher level of offense to suggest that He might actually bring about something we perceive to be negative. But

God *is* sovereign, and while we often pay lip service to His sovereignty, in reality, we desire that His exercising that sovereignty pass our supreme wisdom and foresight. That is, we will allow God to be sovereign as long as His sovereign choices fit our notion of a good and loving God.

Here again is the tendency to create God in *our* image and likeness, and it seems to be a recurring stumbling block. Consequently, as matter of course, we prefer to sidestep the moments in Scripture that demonstrate God's "God-ness," as in the story of the man born blind and so many other narratives in the Bible.

When Pharaoh is viewed in the Old Testament context in isolation of further revelation, he seems to be a belligerent, strong-willed dolt whose spirit is just hard to break. But the Apostle Paul uses Romans 9 to stretch our understanding of God's involvement in the affairs of man.

> For the Scripture says to Pharaoh, "For this very purpose I raised you up, to demonstrate my power in you, and that my name might be proclaimed throughout the whole earth."
>
> Romans 9:17

When referring to Jacob and Esau, God made a choice to favor one over the other before they were ever born. And in the amazing way only the Bible can, it anticipates our emotional/philosophical hiccup with the notion of God actually exercising His will as He desires. Paul, writing in the Spirit, asks, "What shall we say then? There is no injustice with God, is there? May it never be! For He says to Moses, 'I will have mercy on whom I have mercy, and I will have compassion on whom I have compassion'" (Romans 9:14–15).

So God allowing or even designing a baby to come into the world with a birth defect that God will use uniquely for His glory is not only permissible but should be expected as God's rightful prerogative. While we might chafe at the suggestion, God's sovereign capacity is never capricious but only ever an extension of His loving nature whose mercy and grace He desires to lavish on all mankind.

The man born blind entered the world in both spiritual and physical darkness, unable to perceive either physical or spiritual illumination. But spiritual darkness is much more difficult to discern than physical darkness. We can readily detect someone stumbling about with a visual impairment; not so with spiritual impairment. So Jesus uses His power over the physical realm, which is readily observable to our sensory abilities, to demonstrate His power over the spiritual realms—realms into which our sensory abilities are keenly limited.

This point was deemed important enough that the Holy Spirit made sure Jesus's healing the paraplegic was recorded in three of the Gospels.

> "Which is easier, to say to the paralytic, 'Your sins are forgiven'; or to say, 'Get up, and pick up your pallet and walk'? "But so that you may know that the Son of Man has authority on earth to forgive sins"—He said to the paralytic, "I say to you, get up, pick up your pallet and go home."
>
> Mark 2:9–11

Obviously, anyone can stroll up to someone and say, "Your sins are forgiven." While we might have strong, subjective reactions to such a statement, there is no objective, empirical, scientific way of determining whether his sins have been forgiven on our command or not. But if I walk up to a person with a limb previously removed in an accident and I declare, "Leg, grow back!" it will be readily apparent whether I am someone with a special gift or a lunatic.

Today's prophets of health and wealth have a skewed focus altogether. Even where we might assume a genuine healing, many of the prosperity preachers diligently shine the spotlight on the change in a person's physical condition and that is the end of it. But with the healing of the paraplegic, the point of the miracle wasn't that a man who was cursed with an inferior or undesirable physical state was given a better lot in life. The meaning of the miracle had little to do with the man or his condition and everything to do with Jesus, His authority, and who He was. And who Jesus was needed to be accentuated and highlighted in preparation for the greater purposes that were facing Him on the road to redeeming mankind.

In John's passage, it seems possible that God brought a baby into the world by design who was blind, and at another time he faced the man who was paralyzed, it seems, by default. Jesus effects the miraculous in both cases, not solely or even primarily to alleviate the person's inconvenience or suffering, *but to use His creation as tools for His grander purposes.* And we must never lose sight that His purposes are always *good,* whether we understand them at the time or not.

"For My thoughts are not your thoughts, Nor are your ways My ways," declares the LORD. "For as the heavens are higher than the earth, So are My ways higher than your ways And My thoughts than your thoughts."

Isaiah 55:8–9

When we create God in our image and likeness, it is easy, even natural, for us to stand in judgment of God. And that is always a losing proposition.

So Jesus, the *Light* of the world, steps into a world blindsided by sin, taking the man who was born blind from darkness into the light. And while the healing of such physical impairments is considered by most of us a greater challenge to a God who is all-powerful, the fact is that bringing the person steeped in spiritual darkness into the "Light" of His truth, is more challenging (in a manner of speaking) for a loving God who will not trample on man's freedom to choose.

Philip Yancey, in his stellar work, *Disappointment with God*, opens the flood gates of the profound, writing:

> The fact that love does not operate according to the rules of power may help explain why God sometimes seems shy to use his power. He created us to love him, but his most impressive displays of miracle—the kind we may secretly long for—do nothing to foster that love. As Douglas John Hall put it, "God's problem is not that God is not able to do certain things. God's problem is that God loves. Love complicates the life of God as it complicates every life."[14]

So why is it that the peddlers of prosperity are hopelessly mired in the quicksand of fleeting physical benefit rather than the eternal priorities of spiritual fulfillment?

8

THE PROBLEM
OF THE PRESENT
PURSUIT OF PARADISE

Turn on the multitude of "prosperity preachers" and observe their antics for only a few minutes. Their focus is rarely, if ever, on changed hearts but on changed circumstances. What kinds of "miracles" are celebrated: the stubborn gossip brought to repentance, the wife beater broken and contrite, the sex addict liberated from his chains of perversion? Or the woman with migraines miraculously pain-free, the arthritic man healed, the heart attack victim renewed, or the leg grown longer by an inch?

As I watch the shows being incessantly broadcast to thousands upon thousands of unsuspecting hopefuls, their emphasis is clearly on the now instead of the not yet, the miracle instead of the Miracle Giver. Everything revolves around what God wants to do for *you today*. One such preacher's website states:

> In the same service, a woman came forward whose
> eyes were clouded with cataracts. She could barely

see, but after the prayer minister prayed for her, the white glaze over her eyes was gone, and she said her eyesight was great. Another man came off the oxygen tank he had been attached to for months. Deaf ears were opened; cancers were cured; and backs were healed. Hallelujah![15]

We don't need to be steeped in the trappings of prosperity preaching to fall prey to its ruse. Peruse your church's prayer list or perhaps your own prayer list, for that matter, and note where your intercessory priorities fall. If we are honest with ourselves, there is a longing for the message of prosperity deeply seated in all of us. Part of that desire is holy and is grounded in God's promises. This is the kernel of truth that is abused so readily by the prosperity preachers that enables them to obtain so much traction. But beyond the kernel of truth, the bulk of such desire is selfish. The peddlers of prosperity take advantage of this desire, taking the glorious promises of God *for the future* and selling them as entitlements for the Christian *now*.

The Peddlers of Prosperity

For the last several years, I have been listening here and there to broadcasts over the plethora of offerings via satellite. In boredom or exasperation over the abundance of channels and still so little to watch, I will skip in and out from ministry to ministry, preacher to preacher. Then I'll leave it for several weeks or even months, returning periodically to see what is being peddled in the name of Christ.

Amazingly, I have been doing this for several years, yet no matter what time of day, no matter who the individual is, no matter how many weeks or months have lapsed since the last time I jumped in to see what was happening, the message, the ambience, the staging, and the shtick remain the same. The message is clearly one that is foreign to Scripture. A parody of John Kennedy's famous "Ask not" quote serves the prosperity preachers well. "Ask *not* what you can do for God; ask what God can do for you!" Such a god is not the God of Scripture but a god made and worshiped in our image and likeness.

If you've seen one, you truly have seen them all. A preacher is sitting at his desk, holding what he calls the "green prosperity prayer cloth." He prays a prayer of faith for the viewers and then testimonies about the prayer cloth follow. Selecting people from the audience, their stories of prosperity flow.

One woman followed the instructions after receiving the green prosperity prayer cloth, and God gave her a $7,000 financial windfall. Another woman went from a job paying $10 an hour to over $32 an hour. "How many of you would like to triple your income," the preacher asks, "in Jesus's name?"

The camera switches to another couple. Two days after receiving the green prosperity prayer cloth, the man got a better job. They now drive a Lincoln Continental, and they just got a brand-new home. More testimonies about the amazing prosperity prayer cloth flow. A woman with congestive heart failure took her prayer cloth and slept on it. She went to her cardiologist, and he confirmed that she was healed.[16]

The preacher is shown back at his desk, talking softly and somberly, his words dripping with "faith." He holds the prayer cloth up on the screen and asks viewers to put their hand on it "for your health and for your prosperity." He tells the camera that he will pray. He scrunches his eyes shut with a posture of deep faith and prays, releasing "God's blessing of prosperity and health": "My friend," he says, "I feel so good. Start looking for your answer..."

The show concludes with some announcer spouting all the ministry gibberish you hear at the end of a broadcast, concluding with "[We're] spreading the Gospel of Jesus around the world." It was the only time I heard His name uttered, except as a trite ending to another demand sent God's way.[17]

I switch stations to hear two ladies chatting about a "letter from a woman who hasn't gotten her prayer" (healing for her situation) yet. One woman seated opens her Bible and reads a short and incomplete passage from the book of James.

> Is anyone among you sick? Then he must call for the elders of the church and they are to pray over him, anointing him with oil in the name of the Lord; and the prayer offered in faith will restore the one who is sick...
>
> James 5:14–15

After reading, she lapses right into prayer, saying, "Lord we know you want to heal her..." and then proceeds to spell out her demands on the Maker of heaven and Earth, Who is obviously at her beck and call.[18]

There is no rational context for the way the segment of James is used—or better, abused—by the women, but when it comes to prosperity preaching, biblical theology only gets in the way.

One week later, I was again scanning the veritable landfill of prosperity promises. I settled on another prosperity preacher looking into the camera, holding a nearly miniscule vial of "miracle water." He says, "People put it on their open sores, and they dry up. People with internal problems drink it, and suddenly, they realize they don't have that pain anymore! The great thing about this is its *free!*" he explained. "You've never heard me ask for money. My faith is sufficient! I use the water as a point of contact to release your faith." (This might be true regarding his television broadcast offer, but scanning the Internet, there are reports of people who have tried to obtain certain offers from this ministry and found all kinds of strings, costly strings, attached to the "free" offers.)

The scene shifted to a conference setting where this preacher was getting the crowd whipped into a faith frenzy. He said to a man seated in front of him that he saw an angel standing behind him and the angel put his hands on him and touched his heart. He declared the man was healed of whatever his heart problem was as his wife sat beside him, weeping tears of joy.

He handed the vial of miracle water to a woman in the audience. He told her to stretch her legs out and then stated, "You have forty-seven and a half pounds of fluid in your body, and it's all contaminated." He told her to "fast for thirty days and drink nothing but this water! You will purify your system, and you will live twenty-five years longer." He pulled the woman out of her chair—she was a rather voluminous woman—and she began to gingerly hobble around, which, by the increase of decibels of the preacher's voice, was supposed to mean something wonderful, but the connection was never made.

Abruptly, the camera shifted to the preacher speaking to a young woman wearing a patch near her collarbone, telling her she had a biopsy as he was looking to her to confirm that was indeed why she was wearing a patch. She nodded. He continued. "You don't have the results yet, but you're worried about it." Vigorously, he shouted, "I curse cancer," and then smacked her on the forehead as she fell backward into the waiting arms of some assistants.

The camera and scene changed, and the preacher was seated back at his desk, talking to the camera about an *Inside Edition* feature where they came to prove he was a fake. He explained, "But they couldn't do it," and continued to talk about how they wanted to interview him after one of his shows but he wouldn't allow it, saying that he wasn't going to have an "atheist bastard" do the interview with him. He explained to his viewers that the epithet he used was biblical. "That's an unbeliever, according to the Bible," he said. "And if the Lord said it, why can't I?" He was quite tickled with himself as he noted that he had the "courage" to say that, knowing he was being taped.[19]

The "Now" Versus the "Not Yet"

While the manifestations of the prosperity gospel might show themselves with nuanced differences from one preacher to the next, the differences fall basically on where the particular preacher's emphasis is placed. Some lean toward healing of physical ailments, while others tip toward lifestyle or economic issues. Regardless of the particular thrust of any prosperity preacher, their promises all derive from the same flaw in biblical understanding—namely, what *is* the gospel, and what was the purpose of Jesus coming the *first* time compared to why He will come the second time? If you confuse the essence of the gospel, everything else that flows from it will necessarily be confused as well.

The glorious reason the Bible (both Old and New Testaments) was given to us is precisely to spell out for mankind that we have a pernicious flaw at a soul-deep level called *sin*.

From Genesis to Revelation, God explains that man's decision to believe in himself rather than believe in God brought on the destruction of God's perfect plan for universal peace, universal wellness, universal joy, and universal prosperity—not just for mankind, but for the whole created order.

Paul's words to the Roman believers speak to a day—a *day that is yet to be revealed*—when creation itself *will be* (future tense) redeemed or healed from the effects of sin. While that day is a certainty, that day is *not* today.

> For the creation was subjected to futility, not willingly, but because of Him who subjected it, in hope that the creation itself also will be set free from its slavery to corruption into the freedom of the glory of the children of God.
>
> Romans 8:20–21

The gospel is the magnanimous, miraculous events orchestrated by God from before the foundations of the

WILLIAM E. CRIPE, SR.

Earth to redeem mankind for Himself. Since mankind would forfeit the opportunity to live forever in a perfect environment, in perfect relationship with God, God already had a plan to rescue us for Himself.

There are essentially two epochs[1] to the gospel. The first epoch is when Jesus—God in human form—came to deal with the singular issue of man's sin (a desire for autonomy), which is what ruined God's plan for paradise on Earth, turning it upside down. It is man's sin that separates man from God, and it is man's sin that opened the biological gateway for genetic mutation, bringing with it all manner of anatomical/physiological/psychological dysfunction. It is man's sin that tumbled the barriers of perfection that formerly precluded the pathogenesis of harmful microorganisms. It is man's sin that caused man to become self-absorbed and all that that means. While it is certainly true that Satan had a part in the downfall of man, it must not be confused, as another prosperity preacher implies, that Satan and sin are one and the same.

Perusing the above preacher's website after witnessing his prosperity poppycock on the television, I camped on an article he wrote entitled "Faith for Healing Is Based on Knowledge."

In one paragraph, he illustrates numerous theological errors that are at the very heart of prosperity teaching.

---

[1] The gospel is so encompassing and utterly unfathomable in all its wondrous penetrations of our existence that anything stated about what the gospel is will be inadequate. This is not meant to be comprehensive. But since my focus is pertaining to the prosperity gospel, I am spotlighting the aspects of the gospel particularly focused on the errors of prosperity.

As you read the following from the same preacher, remember, if something is true according to God's Word, then it is universally true. This means that if the promises and declarations that issue from the mouths of the peddlers of prosperity are true, they will hold true not only for Christians in the already-prosperous United States but also for God's children in the Sudan. If the tenets of prosperity preaching are true for Christian Europeans, they must also be true for Christian Haitians just the same.

The preacher writes, "Here's another indispensable basic truth you must know and understand about healing: It's never God's will for us to be sick; He wants every person healed every time. That's nearly-too-good-to-be-true news, but that's the gospel."[20]

Is his sound-good, feel-good assertion consistent with biblical revelation? No. The gospel is *not* that God wants to heal everyone here and now or that no one should ever be sick here and now. There are eons of human history that undermine such a preposterous assertion and billions of graves that likewise testify to the absurdity of this preacher's "truth."

If God's intention was to heal every person every time, surely within the sweep of human history there would be some—dare I say, many—who would have been able to apprehend, meaning experience such a routine truth/promise as asserted by the likes of the prosperity peddlers. Certainly the prosperity peddlers themselves should be experiencing such triumph. And yet we know of no one, except Elijah, Enoch, and Jesus—all three arguably exceptional—who have escaped the ultimate physical ravages of sin, resulting in sickness and ultimately death as the penalty of sin.

Elijah and Enoch were not exempt from a faulty physiology because of faith, knowledge, miracle water, or a prayer cloth but by the sovereign will of God Almighty. That is His prerogative. That leaves Jesus, who, in fact, defeated sickness and death as the sole example of what the prosperity preachers want to confer on anyone who just believes hard enough, strong enough, long enough.

But even Jesus didn't conquer bodily breakdown and death "through knowledge," as this preacher describes. He conquered it by being sinlessly perfect. Since "the wages of sin is death," death facing a sinless Savior had no ability, no legal right to claim Jesus's anatomical humanity through physiological breakdown.

More important, beyond the weight of historical evidence to the contrary that, "It's never God's will for us to be sick; He wants every person healed every time," is the perspicuity of scripture itself. This is where the message of the prosperity peddlers meets its demise.

Again, the peddler of prosperity categorically asserts that healing (as a promise of the gospel) is "based on knowledge." If this is true, then such a promise is beyond the sphere of possibility for anyone lacking the intellectual capacity to obtain that knowledge. This means that this particular promise of the gospel is out of reach for infants, the mentally challenged, and the elderly suffering from any number of disease processes afflicting the mind.

He continues his teaching as cited in his *Faith for Healing Is Based on Knowledge*.

It's never God's will for us to be sick…Most Christians don't know or believe that. They think the Lord makes them sick, or at the very least, He allows Satan to make them sick to either punish or correct them. That kind of thinking will get you killed; it's not what the Bible teaches.

Let's consider this assertion in light of biblical revelation.

9

THE PROBLEM OF JOB
FOR THE PEDDLERS
OF PROSPERITY

The Bible doesn't quite affirm the theology of prosperity regarding riches, health, happiness, God, and Satan. Poor old Job received the kind counsel from his "friends" that he might receive today from the peddlers of prosperity. Instead of being pleased, God straightens out Job's friends under threat of death if they do not quit spewing their errant explanations concerning why he was suffering so.

The preacher I mentioned earlier patently denies that God would ever allow Satan to make someone sick, and yet that is exactly what took place in the life of this godly man, Job. Here is Job's story.

> Now there was a day when the sons of God came to present themselves before the LORD, and Satan also came among them. The LORD said to Satan, "From where do you come?" Then Satan answered the LORD and said, "From roaming about on the earth and walking around on it." The LORD said to

Satan, "Have you considered My servant Job? For there is no one like him on the earth, a blameless and upright man, fearing God and turning away from evil." Then Satan answered the LORD, "Does Job fear God for nothing? Have You not made a hedge about him and his house and all that he has, on every side? You have blessed the work of his hands, and his possessions have increased in the land. But put forth Your hand now and touch all that he has; he will surely curse You to Your face." Then the LORD said to Satan, "Behold, all that he has is in your power, only do not put forth your hand on him." So Satan departed from the presence of the LORD.

Job 1:6–12

Anyone who struggles with the reality of a God who might actually exercise His sovereignty in ways that rub one the wrong way, the book of Job will give them fits. There is no side-stepping the clarity of what is taking place. It is a book the peddlers of prosperity need to first read, and then study, and then acknowledge what is clear. It is pointedly contrary to the very hallmarks of what they preach.

Unbeknownst to Job, there is something taking place in the spirit realm to which he is oblivious. It is as if there is a match taking place between God and Satan and God challenges Satan to a spiritual duel. (Pardon the crass nature of my paraphrase, as well as some mild speculation.) Implicit in Satan's statement is that he has been cruising the earth, wreaking havoc on the lives of people and perhaps particularly on people of faith. God steps in, asking, "What about Job? You know, Satan, for some, there is a reality to living by faith that enables a person to look beyond the present nastiness of the daily inequities of life and still live honorably to Me."

Satan takes issue with the objective veracity of God's words and protests, saying, "The only reason Job is faithful is because you have sheltered him, you have increased his holdings, you have shown yourself to be his heavenly benefactor. Who wouldn't stay a fan? But take away your protections from all he possesses, withhold your blessings, remove his prosperity, and watch how quickly he reviles you."

And God says, "You're on! The one restriction I am placing on you is that you may not touch him physically."

The very least one must concede is that God allowed Satan to pilfer Job's prosperity, with the exception of his health. And as the story progresses, Job loses virtually everything, including his family.

The first to go were all of Job's oxen, donkeys, and the people who tended to them. While there might have been some historical contraction in the narration, the way it is presented makes it sound as if this pretty much all happened in the same day. Whether it did or did not is irrelevant. It serves to show a cataclysmic piling-on, if you will, highlighting the extent to which Job's earthly possessions were ravaged.

The next to go were Job's caretakers of the sheep, as well as his flocks. Then the camels and more servants were killed or stolen, and finally, the text says, a great wind took down his eldest son's house, killing all of Job's children.

If it wasn't for the setup at the outset of the book, it would look like Job was the victim of some very bad luck. An external view of Job's situation makes it look like all his calamities are the product of natural disasters or robbery and murder. But we have already been told that this was a divine setup to prove something. So what was the outcome to phase one of this horrific test?

> Then Job arose and tore his robe and shaved his head, and he fell to the ground and worshiped. He said, "Naked I came from my mother's womb, and naked I shall return there. The LORD gave and the LORD has taken away. Blessed be the name of the LORD."
>
> Job 1:19–21

In almost editorial fashion, the conclusion to phase one of the test is announced: "Through all this Job did not sin nor did he blame God" (Job 1:22).

Remember, Job's was an agrarian culture. The NASDAQ and the NYSE were nowhere in sight. One's prosperity was tied up in the land he owned and the produce and livestock his land would support. Job was effectively wiped out. All his hard work, all his building toward security, and all those closest to him were gone. All he had were his health and his wife, and given the response of Job's wife to his calamity, her being spared might also have been part of Job's tragedy.

The same basic scenario of chapter 1 is repeated in chapter 2—God: 1, Satan: 0—but phase two of this supernatural joust is about to begin. This time, Satan complains that while Job might have handled the loss of loved ones and the utter annihilation of economic prosperity, he definitely would not remain faithful to God if God removed the limitation He had placed on Satan in phase one concerning Job's physical being.

The Lord said to Satan, "Have you considered My servant Job? For there is no one like him on the earth, a blameless and upright man fearing God and turning away from evil. And he still holds fast his integrity, although you incited Me against him to ruin him without cause." Satan answered the Lord and said, "Skin for skin! Yes, all that a man has he will give for his life. However, put forth Your hand now, and touch his bone and his flesh; he will curse You to Your face." So the Lord said to Satan, "Behold, he is in your power, only spare his life."

Job 2:3–6

In both phase one and phase two, an interesting conundrum known in philosophy as proximate and ultimate cause is put on display. Proximate cause is the thing or person that is closest in proximity to making something happen, whereas the ultimate cause is more distant to a situation but the initial reason or cause of something happening.

For example, the driver of a vehicle running a red light and smashing into another car would be the proximate cause of the accident. But one could argue that if the man didn't have a car to drive, he couldn't have caused the accident. Therefore, the maker of the car is the real cause of the accident. In this overly simplified and somewhat coarse illustration, the driver is the proximate cause and the manufacturer is the ultimate cause of the accident.

In phase one, paraphrasing Job 1:11–12, Satan says to God, "But put forth *Your* hand now and [*You*] touch all that he has; he will surely curse You to Your face. Then the Lord said to Satan, Behold, all that he has is in *your* power, only [*you*] cannot put forth your hand on him [*physically*]" (emphasis mine).

At the outset Satan wishes for God to do the afflicting, yet God instead gives Satan permission to afflict Job. In phase two, a nearly identical display of proximate and ultimate cause emerges. Satan says, "…[*You God*] put forth *Your hand* now, and touch his bone and his flesh; he will curse You to Your face." God doesn't budge, saying, "Behold, he is in *your* power, only [*you*] spare his life" (Job 2:5–6, emphasis mine).

In both phase 1 and phase 2, the boundaries are laid, and while it might be a bit uncomfortable to us, it certainly suggests Satan is the proximate cause and God the ultimate cause.

> Then Satan went out from the presence of the Lord and smote Job with sore boils from the sole of his foot to the crown of his head. And he took a potsherd to scrape himself while he was sitting among the ashes.
>
> Job 2:3–8

With Job's health now gone on top of everything else, he has nothing but the ill-timed and ill-toned verbal daggers of his sensitive "helpmate."

> Then his wife said to him, "Do you still hold fast your integrity? Curse God and die!"
>
> Job 2:9

Job's response is phenomenal.

> But he said to her, "You speak as one of the foolish women speaks. Shall we indeed accept good from

God and not accept adversity?" In all this Job did not sin with his lips.

Job 2:10

God: 2, Satan: 0, and the match is settled for all but poor Job. We tend to forget that we are given a glimpse of omniscience as we are allowed into the background of what has been going on behind the scenes. But Job knows none of what we know. He knows nothing of the match between God and Satan. He knows nothing of the losses that are not at all natural or coincidental or simply bad luck. He only knows what he has experienced, what he has lost, and that while he doesn't understand, he is not about to hold God culpable for any sense of injustice.

> Naked I came from my mother's womb, and naked I shall return there. The LORD gave and the LORD has taken away. Blessed be the name of the LORD.

Job 1:21

What I love about the book of Job is that Job is *real*. If you read only the few passages I cited here, Job looks larger than life, like a mythological creation of a super-spiritual Goody Two-shoes. But for the next thirty-seven chapters, we are allowed to see into his frustrations, his anger, and his passionate desire, even his *demand* for some answers. And what is even more thrilling is that God doesn't really seem to mind Job's humanness. God is big enough to take Job's spouting and spewing, and it seems as if God knows that Job needs to get some things off his chest. God truly does not mind our questions, yet today's prosperity preachers would denigrate such pro-testations as a betrayal of faith. Such betrayals of faith become the convenient explanation why one's demand for healing or for riches is not fulfilled.

In Job's instance, even in the absence of answers, his faith remains intact. Even while incensed at his rotten string of misfortune, and before he is given any response from God one way or another, Job declares:

> As for me, I know that my Redeemer lives, And at the last He will take His stand on the earth. Even after my skin is destroyed, Yet from my flesh I shall see God; Whom I myself shall behold, And whom my eyes will see and not another. My heart faints within me!
>
> Job 19:25–27

Job had an accurate understanding of God. But even having an accurate understanding of God combined with an equally accurate view of an unjust world is still no salve to an aching soul. For the bulk of the book, Job is trying to figure out what so many of us wrestle with in any number of situations; "Why, God?" And his "friends" come to him with the sincerest of motives but armed with a faulty view of prosperity and a presumptuous view of God. Consequently, what they offer as comfort is an obscene distortion of how God operates in the world when it comes to disappointment.

Each of Job's friends insists that Job had done something to offend God because the underlying foundation of their counsel is that bad things just don't happen to good people. Therefore, their cure for all his woes was for him just to own up to whatever it was he had done and apologize to the Almighty, and his prosperity would return.

Fortunately for us, God made sure we, the readers of history, understood that Job was *not* suffering for anything he had done or failed to do.

"There is no one like him on the earth, a blameless and upright man, fearing God and turning away from evil" (Job 1:8). If you miss that, you can easily miss the wonder of the book.

While God's revelation to us raises many other questions about God, His sovereignty, the spirit realm, and so on, His response categorically removes one problem from the equation. Clearly, Job's friends and their assumptions that Job must have been suffering because he had messed up were flat wrong. The injustices of life, the heartache and sorrow we experience on Earth, do not necessarily spawn from the sufferer having a lack of faith, making poor choices, or worse.

I am not a big fan of poems, but occasionally one is so profound that I am compelled to repeat it. In a few words, this one portrays the right perspective and place of suffering in the lives of faithful people.

> When God wants to drill a man,
>
> And thrill a man,
>
> And skill a man,
>
> When God wants to mold a man
>
> To play the noblest part;
>
> When He yearns with all His heart
>
> To create so great and bold a man
>
> That all the world shall be amazed,
>
> Watch His methods, watch His ways!
>
> How He ruthlessly perfects

Whom He royally elects!

How He hammers him and hurts him

And with mighty blows converts him

Into trial shapes of clay which

Only God understands

While his tortured heart is crying

And he lifts beseeching hands!

How He bends but never breaks

When his good He undertakes;

How He uses whom He chooses,

And which every purpose fuses him;

By every act induces him

To try His splendor out—

God knows what He's about.

—Anonymous

This was Job's condition; the Master Craftsman of our souls at work in the lives of one of His own.

It takes us some forty chapters to see that Job's God is the omnipotent, omnipresent, benevolent, consummately just Creator of the universe Who is not obligated to answer to anyone and might, in fact, decide *not* to. But He is nonetheless the awesome, wondrous Creator of all there is, and He is to be venerated, even when He cannot be comprehended.

God is to be worshiped because of Who He is, not because of what He does or does not do within agreement of our puny, myopic field of view. God is *God*, and Job is not, and that is all Job needed to know.

Even in the book of Job, which is considered to be the earliest books of the Bible, this defining illustration has not dispelled the recurrence of the unfortunate mindset that there is always a causal relationship between behavior and suffering.

The peddlers of prosperity are successfully selling—sometimes literally—a god that is far too human and far too domesticated to be the Lord God Almighty. The god they present appeals to the self-centered, self-absorbed, fleshly component of our being—a component that is present within all of our minds but hopefully is being transformed into the image and likeness of Jesus rather than the other way around.

"But Job is Old Testament," some may protest.

"I am a New Testament child of the King."

"The work of Christ at Calvary hadn't been accomplished yet for people of the Old Testament, like Job."

"As children of the King, we New Testament Christians need to assert our proper place on Earth and demand our rights as royalty!" This is an appealing axiom of the proponents of prosperity. Appealing or not, it is simply wrong.

10

THE PRECARIOUS NATURE OF PROSPERITY PROOF TEXTING

Where the prosperity gospel falters is that its development from the Scriptures is in utter ignorance of any semblance of systematic biblical theology. It fails to understand the Bible as a whole; it fails to allow the Bible to interpret the Bible. Jumping in and out of books, chapters, and verses with utter disregard for context in the immediate, with respect to the whole revelation of God to mankind, is the root of all aberrant beliefs in every age. What makes them so pernicious is that there is almost always a bit of truth contained within the proof texts giving them an air of plausibility. Reading the Bible in this way really does afford someone the ability to prove anything they want from the Bible. And when you combine this façade of biblical legitimacy with a message that appeals to the inherent fallen nature of man, you have a potent setup for deluding the masses.

As a columnist for the central Maine newspapers for nearly a decade, I wrote a bi-weekly op-ed piece called "Looking Up." It wasn't a religion column per se but rather a view of current events from a pointedly biblical frame of reference—that is, by evaluating the world down here by looking up, in other words, from God's vantage point.

I was told by four editors during my time with the papers that my column generated more letters than all of their opinion columns combined. It was always amusing to me how rabidly intolerant and narrow-minded the so-called tolerant and open-minded were when it came to anything that challenged their thinking. That was to be expected. What I wasn't ready for were the "Christians" who would write in with vitriol, disagreeing with many of "my" thoughts, which were nothing more than centuries-old orthodoxy. The "faith once for all delivered to the saints," for which Jude appeals to all believers to contend, has become a free-for-all of subjectivism on the playground of opinions. We can no longer make assumptions about even the most basic of Christian doctrine. In today's culture, non-Christians certainly, but also Christians, are woefully ignorant of the Bible.

To illustrate this, consider an article I wrote about a gathering of women from a broad spectrum of predominantly mainline "Christian" denominations gathering to *re-imagine* the faith.

I wrote (for May 16, 1994):

> This past November women from a broad spectrum of religious denominations gathered together in Minneapolis to "Re-imagine" God and religion.

This conference involving Lutherans (ELCA), Catholics, United Church of Christ and several other churches was sponsored primarily by the Presbyterian Church (USA) and United Methodist Church. Billed as a global theological conference, it is possibly the most blasphemous attempt in history at redefining Christianity.

Susan Cyre, a press observer writing for the Presbyterian Layman, called "Re-imagining 93" a "Feminist convocation declaring their allegiance to the goddess Sophia…destroying the traditional Christian faith, adopting ancient pagan beliefs, rejecting Jesus' divinity and his atonement on the cross, creating a god(dess) in their own image, and affirming lesbian lovemaking…"

Aruna Gnanadason of the World Counsel of Churches proclaimed a "new theological vision of women emerging in every region of the world that is symbolic of the presence of the feminine spirit. And I believe she is here with us. The call is for the reconstruction of some central theological symbols, for example the image of God and the significance of the cross. In a global context where violence and use of force have become the norm, the violence that the cross symbolizes and the patriarchal image of an almighty invincible Father God needs to be challenged and reconstructed."

Delores Williams, Professor at Union Theological Seminary did precisely that. "I don't think we need a theory of atonement at all," said Williams. "I think Jesus came for life and to show us something about life…I don't think we need folks hanging on crosses and blood dripping and weird stuff…" And lesbian feminist Virginia Mollenkott lectured, that "Jesus' death was the ultimate in child abuse and a model for human child abuse. As an incest survivor," she continued, "I can no longer worship in a theological context that depicts God as an abusive parent and Jesus as the obedient trusting child."

In one short conference, Jesus' whole purpose in coming to Earth was discarded as "weird stuff." Cyre again writes, "Chinese feminist Kwok Pui-Lan told conference participants that 'the Chinese reject the Christian belief in the depravity of all human beings who can only be reconciled with God through the death of Jesus the Christ…We cannot have one Savior…Just like the Big Mac… prepackaged and shipped all over the world. It won't do. It's imperialistic.'"

It is not merely arrogant for Kwok to speak for the nation of China but is factually errant in light of the 50 million Chinese Christians who have put their lives and freedom on the line for that Savior who shed His blood for their redemption. Apparently Jesus was misinformed when He announced unambiguously, "No one comes to the Father but by Me."

Chung Hyun Kyung, Assistant Professor in Theology in Seoul noted, "When I think Buddha died when he was in his 80's and Jesus when he was 33—maybe in my Christology book Jesus should be called, 'too young to understand.'" (Laughter followed.) It seems it was not sufficient to simply re-imagine a new, feminized belief system. Conferees also enjoyed mocking the Savior of the world.

With Jesus out of the way Sophia was enthroned by her feminist idolaters. In a special communion service participants recited, "Our maker Sophia, we are women in your image, with the hot blood of our wombs we give form to new life…with nectar between our thighs we invite a lover…with our warm body fluids we remind the world of its pleasures and sensations…with the honey of wisdom in our mouths we prophesy a full humanity to all peoples."

This re-imagined religion is nothing less than a blasphemous justification for abject lust and unqualified perversion. Sexual themes dominated the agenda with all roads inevitably leading back to a convenient hedonism. Lesbian evangelist and recent Colby College lecturer Janie Spahr proclaimed, "Sexuality and spirituality have to come together and Church, we're going to teach you."

Unwittingly summarizing the whole conference Mary Hunt, Roman Catholic and co-founder of Women's Alliance for Theology, Ethics and Rituals defiantly announced, "Preoccupation with eternal truth has given way in our time to survival concerns as the defining line for theological reflection and in my imagination we will shed the excess baggage of patriarchy and assume the interwoven stance of a people doing justice or we will die trying. This is what it means to me to be religious. Whether it is Christian or not is frankly, darling, something about which I no longer give a pope."

In this Ms. Hunt was right. "Re-imagining 93" was utterly devoid of truth. Fortunately we still have the eternal Word of God and its admonition is clear.

"Why are the nations in an uproar and the peoples devising a vain thing? The kings of the earth take their stand, and the rulers take counsel together against the Lord and against His Anointed: He who sits in the heavens laughs, the Lord scoffs at them. Then He will speak to them in His anger and terrify them in His fury: Now therefore, O kings, show discernment; Take warning, O judges of the earth. Worship the LORD with reverence, and rejoice with trembling. Do homage to the Son, lest He become angry, and you perish in the way, for His wrath may soon be kindled" (Psalm 2).

My column spawned a landslide of angry letters to the editor and online comments left at the paper's website. They illustrate the utter lack of basic biblical knowledge or respect for the Bible as the inspired, infallible, inerrant, authoritative Word of God. This is the prime reason so many are easily led astray today.

The first letter is from a local physician.

> I consider myself a regular Sunday go-to-meeting kind of person. I often go to church three times a week for choir practice, book group, and Sunday service. Yet according to Bill Cripe, my Methodist church has been condemned because of difference of doctrinal opinion within its ranks…Real conversation about this sacred spiritual essence as expressed by the great wisdom traditions of the world can only lead to a better understanding of god. I greatly prefer the eclectic spirituality of Professor Jenny Boyle[2] to the myopic self-righteousness of Cripe.

The rest of the letters are from people who claim or allude to a personal adherence to some semblance of Christianity.

---

[2] Professor Jenny Boyle is a transgendered local professor at Colby College in Waterville, Maine. Jenny Boyle used to be James Finney Boylan.

The total lack of self-consciousness exhibited by Pastor Bill Cripe in his Aug. 4 column can only cause one to sigh in pity. He seems to excoriate every church but his own and never considers that preachers such as himself may lead Americans to lose faith in religion. He labels himself a "follower of Christ" when he shows no evidence that he has even read the gospels. "Do not judge, so that you may not be judged" (Matthew 7:1); "Why do you see the speck in your neighbor's eye, but do not notice in the log in your own eye?" (Matthew 7:3); "If you wish to be perfect, go, sell your possessions, and give the money to the poor" (Matthew 19:21).

Pastor Bill Cripe is leader of a wacko church in Waterville who busies himself in politics more than religion. He is a perfect example of why the Founding Fathers approved the first amendment to keep these loonies out of politics.

God is about love and acceptance. I don't think he hates any of his children. If we lead a good honest life and treat others with respect and kindness, that's all life should be about. "Pastor" Cripe teaches bigotry and narrow-mindedness. I think he is a very dangerous person.

This one was from a local pastor:

I am a member of a different church from him, but I must say I have enjoyed reading his writings for years, and I can't remember ever disagreeing with him. That is, until the article on Aug. 4. I can only describe it as religion "bashing." The Rev. Bill Cripe's words were used like clubs to attack the religious beliefs of others. Christian supremacism is not "manifest destiny." The world, and our religion, needs understanding, not theological claims to superiority.

Is it any wonder that the prosperity gospel derives it authority from nothing other than "feel good"?

With the intent of reaching others who might be on the fence of rational discourse, I responded personally to one woman whose comments typified the opinion of a broad spectrum of people concerning "religion" and truth. Specifically, that one's personal convictions are what define what is true. She identified herself as a Unitarian. This is what I wrote.

Dear Claire,

I do understand that you don't believe the Bible to be the authoritative Word of God. That is your prerogative just as someone picking up a loaded gun has the prerogative to believe it is not loaded. But one's personal belief does not validate or invalidate the truth. So if you sincerely believe the gun is empty and you pull the trigger of a loaded gun, there will be a discharge of the round within whether you believe it or not.

It is not belief or disbelief that determines truth but One truthful source. That truthful source is God who revealed Himself in the person of Jesus. And even that Jesus is not just any old "Jesus" someone imagines but the Jesus who revealed Himself to the world through incarnation.

Nothing I wrote in my article contradicted anything Jesus said, taught, or demonstrated. So please feel free to disagree, but your disagreement does not alter the truth. Jesus Himself said, "I am the

Way, the Truth, the Life, and no one comes to the
Father but by Me." So your issues of disagreement
are with Him, not me. Please seek Him out in the
pages of the Bible; there is no other book like it.

That North American people in general and Christians
in particular are ignorant of the contents of the Bible
is born out year after year by research conducted by
Gallup, Barna, and the Pew organization. The authority of Scriptures has also been upended by our culture of
individualism. Many of today's Christians are primed to
stake their lives—perhaps literally—on what the Bible
"says to them," and what the Bible says to them trumps
all else. Centuries of scholarship, principles of interpre-
tation, and sound methodology of inquiry is something
of a previous era. In our world today, *I* am the final
authority.

On my first day of class at Trinity Evangelical
Divinity School, Dr. Walter Kaiser introduced his course
with a humorous description of many of today's Bible
studies. The following is a paraphrase of his all-too-true
discourse.

You might have experienced a discussion group or
Bible study where someone with the title of facilitator
moderated—they didn't teach, heaven forbid; that would
be too authoritarian or might smack of pride. So the
facilitator facilitated the pooling of everyone's thoughts
with all thoughts being equal. So it began with the facilitator throwing out a verse or a passage to the group and
then saying, "What does this say to you?" Usually after
an awkward silence, someone, boldly, said something
like, "Well, to *me,* it means…" to which the facilitator
responded gently, saying, "Oh, that's interesting."

You see, it is somehow deemed un-Christian to insinuate someone's understanding is somehow *wrong.*

Then the next person chimed in and said, "Oh, I don't get that at all. To me, it says …" And after everyone who wants to add their "wisdom" is finished, the facilitator moved on to the next passage of the "study."

With biblical illiteracy at a pandemic level across the board, including the church that wears the name of Jesus, it is no wonder that so many people are sucked into the wiles of prosperity preaching. It caters exactly to what we want to hear.

While there are many pet passages that the prosperity peddlers like to camp on, one of the favorites of those who emphasize a prosperity of healing is the famous Isaiah passage that speaks of physical well-being.

I was yet again viewing the offerings of satellite religion, and internationally renowned preacher/prophet/healer Benny Hinn was seated on stage, telling his colleagues the following:

> Don't forget to look at the back of the cross (meaning Jesus's back on the cross) because the back is healing! The front is salvation; we think of salvation when we see the front. But don't settle for fifty percent! Look at the back of Jesus; it's for healing.[21]

Then he went to the Isaiah 53 passage, quoting, "By His stripes we are healed!" With emanations of oooing and ahhing, his infatuated colleagues, who had heard his shtick many times, acted as if it was the first time they had heard something so profound. As they got more and more excited, the prophet/healer continued to explain why more people are not healed. Referring to those who give up, Hinn asked, "Why do we say, 'Take my life'? We should say, 'Take my body. Take my cancer.' He only heals what we give Him."

Nobody ever seemed to question such nonsense. If the preacher was right and we can only be healed of "what we give Him," and if another prosperity preacher I mentioned was right when he asserted that "healing is by knowledge," then each one of us is obligated to be omniscient with respect to our physical and mental health. After all, we can't give to Him that for which we have no knowledge. Hinn's assertion presupposes that we have a comprehensive knowledge of our situation so that we can, in fact, give whatever it is that is ailing us to God. Otherwise, healing will be elusive.

This rationale provides a loophole of sorts for the peddlers of prosperity when someone doesn't obtain whatever it is they have demanded. Like Job's friends, the preachers of prosperity always manage to turn it back on the person, cleverly finding some deficiency in their understanding, their faith, or their methodology. The "name it, claim it" preachers place an awful lot of responsibility on the individual to procure one's "healing." This is an untenable position for a faith grounded in God's initiative, God's mercy, and God's grace.

Returning to Hinn's proof text, one must ask, "Is Isaiah 53 a promise of unequivocal healing for anyone and everyone, as the prosperity preachers insist?" The answer is clear when Isaiah's prophecy is understood in context. It prophesies of the coming Redeemer with beautiful clarity, explaining His purpose in coming.

> Who has believed our message? And to whom has the arm of the LORD been revealed? For He

grew up before Him like a tender shoot, and like a root out of parched ground; He has no stately form or majesty that we should look upon Him, nor appearance that we should be attracted to Him. He was despised and forsaken of men, a man of sorrows and acquainted with grief; and like one from whom men hide their face He was despised, and we did not esteem Him. Surely our griefs He Himself bore, and our sorrows He carried; yet we ourselves esteemed Him stricken, smitten of God, and afflicted. But He was pierced through for our transgressions, He was crushed for our iniquities; the chastening for our well-being fell upon Him, and by His scourging we are healed. All of us like sheep have gone astray, each of us has turned to his own way; But the LORD has caused the iniquity of us all To fall on Him.

Isaiah 53:1–6

Without even going beyond the confines of this passage, it is hard to miss the point of Isaiah's words. It is not some promise that Jesus became the embodiment of our sicknesses, ailments, diseases, or dysfunctions. It is not some promise that, in Jesus's incarnation, every pathogenesis known to mankind has been eliminated. It should be obvious that if any notion of this were true, the faithful would experience perfected bodies, never to succumb to any disease process again.

In fact, Isaiah is affirming that it is our sinfulness that has caused us each to do our own thing, to do what *we* determine to be right in our own eyes. This is our natural tendency from which we need deliverance. But even after we have been delivered, living in a perpetually broken, sin-tainted world has brought upon us the myriad problems we experience in this world. "The wages of sin *is* death," Paul writes to the church at Rome.

Through Isaiah and others, we come to see clearly that sin enrages a holy God; and His wrath against such unholiness cannot simply be swept under a rug without impugning His character, His justice. But amazingly, instead of pouring out His anger on every deserving soul, He instead became a human being in all aspects of our humanity, except that He came free of sin. And His purpose in coming was to live the way life is supposed to be lived by each one of us. He did not come for Himself.

Isaiah 53 is not about the petty healing of what amounts to annoyances and inconveniences in the grand scheme of things. It is about the grand healing of the very core of what afflicts mankind, namely our *sin* nature.

So the first epoch of the gospel shows that when Jesus came to Earth the first time, it was for the purpose of dealing with our sin so that when we die, we will not stay dead. He did not come to correct every wrong brought about by the sinfulness of mankind. Neither did he come to punish every injustice or to erase the pain of living in a broken world. That is what He will do in the next epoch when He returns. This is the hope of every Christian, the day when every knee will bow and every tongue will confess that Jesus is Lord. Then and only then will everything the prosperity preachers are trying to sell as the believer's right for today be realized. But this begs the question: Is it really that harmful? Is it wrong to fill people with optimism, hope, and excitement, even if it stretches the truth a bit? You will be able to answer that when you finish this book.

Prosperity preachers are filling sincere people with false promises or at best ill-timed promises that might be true for a future day but not for now. Not everything we have been granted "in Christ" is meant to be experienced *now*. When Paul writes to the Corinthians about that future day, he is clear about the timing of experiencing the promises of joy, of pain removed, and when sickness will be a thing of the past.

> Behold, I tell you a mystery; we will not all sleep, but we will all be changed, in a moment, in the twinkling of an eye, at the last trumpet; for the trumpet will sound, and the dead will be raised imperishable, and we will be changed. For this perishable must put on the imperishable, and this mortal must put on immortality. But when this perishable will have put on the imperishable, and this mortal will have put on immortality, then will come about the saying that is written, "Death is swallowed up in victory. O death, where is your victory? O death, where is your sting?" The sting of death is sin, and the power of sin is the law; but thanks be to God, who gives us the victory through our Lord Jesus Christ.
>
> 1 Corinthians 15:51–57

As a pastor who has conducted many funerals over the years, it is still irksome when a well-meaning brother or sister tries to comfort the one who has just experienced the loss of their loved one using some careless form of Paul's words in this passage. "John is in a better place! You should be happy for him and rejoicing that he is no longer suffering."

All of that is certainly true—the wonderful kernel of truth—but the Bible doesn't say that there will be no pain in death *now* or that there will be no sorrow in separation. The Bible doesn't say that if we really believed all the wonderful promises of God, even with a sufficient amount of faith, whatever that would be, the loss of loved ones would be a stroll in the park.

Rather, Paul writes:

> But when this perishable will have put on the imperishable, and this mortal will have put on immortality, *then* will come about the saying that is written, "Death is swallowed up in victory. O death, where is your victory? O death, where is your sting?"

Which means right *now*, death *hurts*, death stings, death is an insult, death is not "natural," nor is it a "normal" part of life to which we often hear it glibly referred. Death is the penalty of sin, and it was meant to sting, *but* that sting doesn't smart nearly as much for those who have the promise of the future hope. The *then* in the passage is the *when* the sting will no longer smart, and the *then* is not *now* but when Jesus comes the second time.

Jesus Wasn't Always Feeling Prosperous

Prosperity preachers have an impossible time squaring their vacuous theology with Jesus's own experience of life as a human being. In the famous incident in the life of one of Jesus's old friends, Lazarus, there is a short verse that has been the subject of speculation over the ages. It pertains to Jesus's emotional response at the tomb that day.

> Then the Jews who were with her in the house, and consoling her, when they saw that Mary got up quickly and went out, they followed her, supposing that she was going to the tomb to weep there. Therefore, when Mary came where Jesus was, she saw Him, and fell at His feet, saying to Him, "Lord, if You had been here, my brother would not have died." When Jesus therefore saw her weeping, and the Jews who came with her also weeping, He was deeply moved in spirit and was troubled, and said, "Where have you laid him?" They said to Him, "Lord, come and see." Jesus wept. So the Jews were saying, "See how He loved him!" But some of them said, "Could not this man who opened the eyes of the blind man have kept this man also from dying?"
>
> John 11:31–38

Why did Jesus weep? Why didn't He just apprehend the wonderful promises of the peddlers of prosperity, which say God never intends anyone to be sick? Surely if anyone was capable of tapping into the promises of prosperity, it was Jesus.

Some have said Jesus wept because He was saddened by the lack of faith of the mourners and of Mary and Martha. But that doesn't make much sense. If anything, Mary demonstrates a rather strong faith when she says, "If You had been here, my brother would not have died." The other mourners say pretty much the same thing. But John records that at least one person noted Jesus's tears as evidence of His love for Lazarus.

In my opinion, this is closer to the truth, but I will add my own speculation as to why Jesus might have wept. (And it is speculation because the Word does not tell us plainly.)

Many years ago, I had to attend a funeral as part of my seminary training. I was to do nothing more than observe, and it didn't need to be the funeral of anyone I knew, nor did I have to know anyone who knew the deceased. So I watched the newspaper and found a funeral that would be conducted nearby at a convenient time for me to attend.

I entered the funeral home and sat in the back as the memorial began for the elderly woman who had passed after an illness of some length. In the front row where family sits, there were several teenage girls who were broken up about their grandma having passed away. As the service came to an end, it was time for the people to file by the casket, paying their last respects, and as these teens approached the casket, they fell apart and were actually draping themselves on top of the casket, weeping for their grandma. As I watched, I was moved to tears myself, seeing the sorrow of these girls and the sorrow that death brings into the world. Even though I had no emotional connection to anyone at this service, I was moved to tears, and I remember thinking afterward, *Maybe that is why Jesus wept at the grave of his friend.* It wasn't a despairing, hopeless sorrow, obviously, but death is a hideous insult to the glorious eternity that God had created us all to enjoy in the Garden. So for now, death reminds everyone, even God incarnate, that death has a sting and that the fullness of the glorious redemption of man will not be realized until the second coming, when death is destroyed for all time.

Sometimes Jesus, as a man, makes us uncomfortable. As Christians, we know in theory He was fully human, but it is the "fully God" part we would rather contemplate.

The great kenosis or emptying passage in Philippians 2:5–7, though enigmatic, is marvelous, saying that Jesus clearly took the role of a bond servant of God the Father. Remember, Jesus was fully man while being fully God, and remember that in His manhood, Jesus emptied Himself of at least some of His divine prerogatives (omniscience, for example), instead relying on God, His Father.

So when asked about the timing of His return, Jesus replied, "But of that day and hour no one knows, not even the angels of heaven, nor the Son, but the Father alone" (Matthew 24:36).

Additionally, it seems He also gave up some of His own authority. When Jesus performed His miraculous healings, He did not do so by fiat—at least not by his own fiat—but only as the Father enabled Him to do so.

> One day He was teaching; and there were some Pharisees and teachers of the law sitting there, who had come from every village of Galilee and Judea and from Jerusalem; *and the power of the Lord was present for Him to perform healing.*
>
> Luke 5:17 (emphasis mine)

If it is noted that the power of the Lord was present for Jesus to heal in one instance, it certainly seems to imply that there were times and places when the power of the Lord was not present for Jesus to do much of anything.

I know the common perception of the masses that have been raised in the church is that Jesus did whatever He wanted when He wanted, but Jesus seems to indicate that it wasn't even by His own authority or desire that He worked any miracles at all but rather only as He was compelled as God the Father directed.

> Therefore Jesus answered and was saying to them, "Truly, truly, I say to you, the Son can do nothing of Himself, unless it is something He sees the Father doing; for whatever the Father does, these things the Son also does in like manner."
>
> John 5:19

Considering it all, why did Jesus weep? It doesn't seem unreasonable that Jesus was weeping at the tomb of His friend, Lazarus, because death is a sad affair, even for the One who came to conquer death once for all.

Nevertheless, the peddlers of prosperity are slow to allow their profitable preaching to be informed by the facts of Scripture. Instead, they are promising heaven on Earth now, in all its victory.

11

THE PREDICAMENT OF THE PROSPERITY MESSAGE

The promise of prosperity that demands the experience of heaven while still living on Earth is simply wrong. I believe Christians living in the days of Jesus and thereafter would be surprised to learn that they suffered the way they did because they weren't fortunate enough to grasp the prosperity message as it is peddled by today's hustlers.

I doubt John the Baptist was feeling prosperous in light of his life experience. John's faith and faithfulness were not "blessed" with a scenic cruise or a fat advance for his memoirs. Instead, he was rewarded with a stay at Hotel Herod. When you consider Jesus's glowing compliment about John in Matthew 11:11, one can hardly blame a lack of faith for John's less-than-prosperous experience as often implied by today's prosperity pastors when one's "faith demand" doesn't come to pass. John doesn't plead for a vial of miracle water or send for a prayer cloth. He doesn't even demand release. Instead, he wants some reassurance that his suffering is worthwhile, that it is for the right cause, the right person. But what prompted his desire and need for encouragement? Could it be the collision of John's experience of life in a fallen world against the prophetic words of the Savior? Four chapters into Luke's gospel, Jesus cites a passage from Isaiah 61. Jesus says:

> The Spirit of the Lord is upon me, because he anointed me to preach the gospel to the poor. He has sent me to proclaim release to the captives, and recovery of sight to the blind, to set free those who are oppressed, to proclaim the favorable year of the Lord.
>
> Luke 4:18–19

Jesus concludes His mini lecture, saying, "Today this Scripture has been fulfilled in your hearing" (Luke 4:21).

What? Release to the captives? Freedom to the oppressed? *If this Jesus is the One,* John must have thought, *and He came to set the captives free, how come I'm still in bondage?*

The answer that comes back to John might seem a little disconcerting to the one going through the hard time, but the spirit of God uses it to console his confused heart.

His disciples came to Jesus, saying:

> John the Baptist has sent us to You, to ask, "Are You the Expected One, or do we look for someone else?" At that very time He cured many people of diseases and afflictions and evil spirits; and He gave sight to many who were blind. And He answered and said to them, "Go and report to John what you have seen and heard: the blind receive

sight, the lame walk, the lepers are cleansed, and the deaf hear, the dead are raised up, the poor have the gospel preached to them."

Luke 7:20–22

A paraphrase of Jesus's words would read something like this: "John, think about all you have read about Me, all you have seen about Me, all you have heard about Me, and all the Spirit affirms in your heart about Me. All these things speak to your soul, affirming to you that 'I AM.' I AM the One who came to take away your sins, and by My righteousness, you have been delivered from all unrighteousness and its sickening consequences. You have been delivered, John, from sin's bondage. You have been delivered from eternal condemnation, and one day—a day yet to come—you will experience the fullness of all that I AM. Remember, My kingdom is *not* of this world. So for now, you are my witness, even unto death."

Not long after, John was beheaded.

The prosperity peddlers might protest, saying Jesus hadn't gone to the cross yet, which is why John wasn't eligible for the prosperity they push. That might work for a recalcitrant few, but the skeptic is still left having to deal with another faithful man who didn't exactly experience the kind of prosperity the hucksters thrive on today. By the time Saul of Tarsus came on the scene, Jesus had been crucified and had already ascended into heaven. So if there are any issues concerning the chronology of the full gospel—i.e., complete fulfillment—and its relationship to the gospel of prosperity, they are upended when Paul's life experiences are considered.

It would be hard to find another human being who put himself more on the line for Jesus than Saul, better known to us as the Apostle Paul. And if there is anything Paul understood, it is that he was a servant of Christ. As His servant, he understood he was to be used by Him, for *His* purposes. Jesus, God, did not come to be Paul's cosmic genie. He did not come to lavish on Paul the world's offerings of reward. Paul gives a good summary of the nature of the prosperity he experienced, not merely since becoming a follower of Jesus but precisely because he became a follower of Jesus.

> Five times I received from the Jews thirty-nine lashes. Three times I was beaten with rods, once I was stoned, three times I was shipwrecked, a night and a day I have spent in the deep. I have been on frequent journeys, in dangers from rivers, dangers from robbers, dangers from my countrymen, dangers from the Gentiles, dangers in the city, dangers in the wilderness, dangers on the sea, dangers among false brethren; I have been in labor and hardship, through many sleepless nights, in hunger and thirst, often without food, in cold and exposure. Apart from such external things, there is the daily pressure on me of concern for all the churches.
>
> 2 Corinthians 11:23–28

What if the faithful followers of Christ, who suffered for most of their lives because of their faith, suddenly appeared in the audiences of today's charlatans, selling what amounts to spiritual snake oil? It seems reasonable that they would be rather shocked at the pretentious demand for God's blessing of perfect health, extraordinary success, and abundant riches *now*. Consider what we are shown regarding Christian faithfulness.

Hebrews 11 is sometimes called "faith's hall of fame." It serves us to contemplate how offensive the foolishness of such promises of a charmed life would be to these faith-filled martyrs. Why didn't they preach that no one need ever be sick or that the faithful should never do without, that the Christian must never be deprived or that God wants us to have all the physical and material success our selfish hearts can imagine? Can you envision their response to the insinuation or outright accusation that their failure to experience the so-called prosperity of this world now was due to a lack of faith? I truly wonder which Bible the patrons of prosperity ever read.

The truly faithful, who the writer of Hebrews describes, have a vastly different experience of life than the people-pleasing prosperites are portraying.

> Others were tortured, not accepting their release, so that they might obtain a better resurrection; and others experienced mockings and scourgings, yes, also chains and imprisonment. They were stoned, they were sawn in two, they were tempted, they were put to death with the sword; they went about in sheepskins, in goatskins, being destitute, afflicted, ill-treated (men of whom the world was not worthy), wandering in deserts and mountains and caves and holes in the ground.
>
> Hebrews 11:35–38

Being a follower of Jesus promised no bed of roses. In fact, more often than not, their life experience was quite the contrary. Even today, precious, faithful Christians around the globe are paying for their faithfulness to Jesus with the prosperity of persecution. Even as I write, friends of mine are in peril every day, living in a closed country where conversion to Christ can mean death.

What every schemer who wears the name of Christ while peddling a self-gratifying gospel needs to see is that *this world was not Jesus's kingdom and this world is not our home.* A challenging experience of life is not an aberration of faith or manifestation of doubt but is exactly the way God planned it. This is why the rest of Hebrews is so powerfully important in exposing the ruse of a popular prosperity.

"And all these [*referring to the highly faithful*], having gained approval through their faith, did *not* receive what was promised, because God had provided something better…" (Hebrews 11:39–40, emphasis mine).

For the Hebrew believers, God's promise for something better is never in doubt. "God had [*already*] provided something better." They were never promised they would necessarily receive it then and there.

This doesn't sound anything like a promise for everyone to receive his or her "best life now." To be promised this world as the reward for a life of faith would be a major rip-off. This world is dying and passing away. One day, it will be completely gone, and a new one—an eternal one—will take its place. That is the world of the faithful's inheritance, not the superficial guarantee of a high-paying job, a new home, or a Mercedes 450 SEL, even one that's paid for. What a cheap sellout, and the peddlers of prosperity are stumbling the masses with great hubris.

Again, from the writer of Hebrews:

All these [*faithful followers of Jesus*] died in faith, without receiving the promises, but having seen them and having welcomed them from a distance, and having confessed that they were strangers and exiles on the earth. For those who say such things make it clear that they are seeking a country of their own. And indeed if they had been thinking of that country from which they went out, they would have had opportunity to return. But as it is, they desire a better country, that is, a heavenly one. Therefore God is not ashamed to be called their God; for He has prepared a city for them.

Hebrews 11:13–16

They did not receive what was promised because God has provided something *better* for us...And that something better for us will be realized later down the eschatological road.

The sort of prosperity promises offered in the counterfeit gospel of prosperity is not the prosperity of "Thy kingdom [will] come" but "Thy kingdom [has] already come."

This kind of prosperity is not obtainable today— at least not in the sense it is proffered. Unfortunately for the masses, the scammers are astoundingly successful. The prosperity preacher peddling his miracle water raked in over $20 million in the past four years.[22]

Most of the prosperity preachers I have referenced here are blatantly obvious in their extremes and abuses. Their theatrical antics seem like a parody of themselves, yet that has not diminished their impact on the naïve, the hurting, or the desperate. Not all are as obvious or as duplicitous though, and consequently, the prosperity gospel has infiltrated mainstream evangelicalism with overwhelming impact.

12

PURSUING A PROSPERITY OF TRUTHFULNESS

I sincerely want to be careful here; hence, the qualifications pertaining to what I am about to write. We live in tumultuous times. We live in both a time of phenomenal technology and also a time of phenomenal burden because of that technology. With the World Wide Web, we have access to the events of the entire planet in real-time. We no longer have to wait to find out about a catastrophic earthquake or the campus shooting a day or two after the fact and that, after it's been analyzed, filtered, and the desired images selected. Instead, we are privy to aerial views from a helicopter in a far-off land we might not have even known existed before. Thanks to technology, we can share in the agony as someone is being pulled from a crushed building in all their dismembered glory.

With cameras on the ground, we are standing beside loved ones, wailing in grief as they observe the horror having hoped their child or father or sister or friend would be found alive. Before the soul-wrenching of that scene has had time to settle, we are instantaneously taken to a more familiar geography in Anywhere, USA.

A child with a grudge has opened fire on his classmates, and thanks to someone's video phone, we are once again privy to the horror as if we are standing on the scene. Thanks to technology, we have achieved a semblance of omniscience. With such a gift comes a huge responsibility, as well as burden, and there is need for tremendous wisdom to utilize it properly.

The problem with having acquired a kind of quasi-omniscience is that we are still only finite beings with a limited capacity to intellectually ponder and emotionally process a virtually unlimited amount of sensory stimulation.

Thanks to e-mail, I can know that my friends on the other side of the world are being surveilled by the government and risk deportation or worse. The prayer chain is activated. But with the ability to also have unsolicited information forced upon me, I can also know—whether I want to or not—that three children of a friend of a coworker of an uncle of someone I once might have known are facing removal from their homes by Human Services due to the sexually abusive boyfriend of the children's drug-abusing mother. And this is truly only the minute tip of a glacier of information available to us every moment of every day.

When God told the first family not to eat of the tree of knowledge of good and evil, He didn't ever say why. But a chapter later, the serpent, whose masterful deceit is deployed by taking a kernel of God's truth, using part of it or twisting it for his purposes, unwittingly gives us insight as to why God forbade them from eating of it.

He hisses, "For God knows that in the day you eat from it your eyes will be opened, and you will be like God, knowing good and evil" (Genesis 3:5).

While our culture prides itself on the acquisition of knowledge—after all, knowledge is power—the truth of the statement is that, while being like God is tantalizing, there is only One who is capable of handling the job. For the rest of us, shouldering even one of the weighty elements of divinity would bury us.

Through technology, I was given the opportunity to talk to a significant portion of New England on a show called *Maine in the Morning*. Once a week, I was on the air live with the show's two hosts, who would bring up whatever issue or event was currently hot anywhere in the world. Usually I never knew what was coming. They would field phone calls from listeners, taking great delight in pelting me, the conservative, religious guy, with anything and everything imaginable. I took my preparation seriously, for it was a tremendous opportunity to bring God's heart and mind to bear in issues of relevance to the listeners. Consequently, my preparation for the show was that, throughout the week, I engulfed myself in every source of news available. I did my best to stay abreast of every imaginable avenue of information that might help me engage a secular culture with the glorious truths of Scripture.

The show lasted a couple years and then ended when the producer of the show moved to a different part of the state. Although I was truly saddened when the opportunity ended, I took a news sabbatical of which the vestiges linger. I hadn't realized what a toll knowing everything that was happening in the world, day in and day out, had taken on me and on those around me.

Our shoulders just are not big enough to carry the weight of omniscience. Eating of the tree of knowledge of good and evil is more than we can bear. Of course, our great God knew that and, out of love for His children, tried to warn us.

With the advent of technology, we are a people on edge, a people who are taken to the height of exultant good news and then right into the pit of hell in a matter of sixty seconds or less. And this is repeated throughout the day, day in, day out, every day of our lives.

So we are a people desperately desirous for good news, wantonly in need of hope, optimistically in need of a fresh vision for a better tomorrow. And the one source for such good news is found in the pages of Scripture. To be sure, there are many conniving individuals garbed with the credibility of a minister of God who, by design, are fleecing the flock. Still, many others are simply trying to encourage people to boost their spirits in these times of predictable disappointment and sorrow.

None of this is to excuse that somewhere along the line, the necessity and hunger for positive news took on a life of its own. When that happened, the purveyor of such a message, with its tangible rewards, increasingly became the servant of the message. Instead of the whole counsel of God's Word being proclaimed, a caricature of the truth emerged. And while that caricature grows in popularity, it is a caricature nonetheless. A desire to bring hope and good news to people is well and good, yet false hope and good news that is contrived will, in the end, crush those it was intended to revive.

The Prosperity Gospel Goes Mainstream

Joel Osteen was a young man operating the cameras for his father's ministry when an unforeseen heart attack took the life of John Osteen. Joel, having never preached before, was thrust into the pulpit as the heir apparent to his father's six-thousand-member church.[23]

Not having finished college and never having attended seminary, one must acknowledge that Pastor Osteen is a gifted and talented individual. With a church of upwards of forty thousand—a number that is hard to comprehend—Osteen is an inherently talented person. He has achieved a place of prominence in the world of evangelicalism, and with such prominence comes examination of the spotlight. Depending on where a spotlight is aimed, it can reveal the beauty of everything that has been prepared for the light. Aimed elsewhere, such penetrating light tends to reveal the not-so-beautiful as well.

Although I spend some time critiquing Pastor Osteen's theology, it is only because he typifies the more respectable and, in some ways, a more covert prosperity message. He also is the most visible of the prosperity peddlers today and, having put his thoughts in writing, invites thoughtful analysis.

Pastor Osteen's first book is the wildly popular *Your Best Life Now: 7 Steps to Living at Your Full Potential*. It has sold over four million books at the time of my writing, which certainly affirms the fact that he has struck a nerve, scratching where people are itching. Osteen has given many people a new optimism and a fresh vision both sorely needed in our day.

Through anecdotal illustrations of the principles of his book, he makes you believe not only that anything (materially) is possible but that fulfillment of your grand imaginations, your most elaborate dreams, is not simply within your grasp but as a Christian is yours by right. Grander still is that there is actually a God on your side who is irretrievably for you. This is great news to be sure and true news most importantly. But the peddlers of prosperity gleefully traipse off the path of biblical truth, diving into an idolatry-based heresy as they incessantly proclaim that this God Who is on your side exists first and foremost to bring those dreams into reality.

While some might find it difficult to identify such a positive, hopeful message as "sinful," Timothy Keller, writing in *The Reason for God*, has a broader view of sin. Using the late philosopher Soren Kierkegaard's definition, Keller explains:

> Most people thinking of sin primarily as breaking divine rules, but Kierkegaard knows that the very first of the Ten Commandments is to "have no other gods before me." So according to the Bible, the primary way to define sin is not just the doing of bad things, but the making of good things into ultimate things. It is seeking to establish a sense of self by making something else more central to your significance, purpose and happiness than your relationship to God.[24]

A god who exists to serve *me* is an appealing concept to be sure. And true to the foundations of the prosperity message, the god Osteen portrays in *Your Best Life Now* is more suited to a genie who lives in a magic lamp found on a beach than the self-existent Creator of the universe. With his prominent success at the expense of truth, Osteen is perhaps today's supreme exemplar of the up-

and-coming prosperity preachers who are undaunted by the whole counsel of Scripture. Conveniently skipping anything that might be culturally or personally offensive is the expected norm. In a quest to be always upbeat and unobtrusively optimistic, the prosperity preachers have compromised the message of redemption. Routinely, the glorious work of Christ, paying the horrific penalty of our sins, is utterly hidden beneath a flowery façade of an insipid language of love. When pressed, the truth of Jesus's sacrifice is so ambiguously approached as to be essentially denied.

On national television, Joel Osteen sat before Larry King and millions of people watching. After a woman called in from Phoenix, citing the passage where Jesus says plainly that He is the Way, the Truth, and the Life and no one comes to the Father but by Him, Mr. King began pressing Pastor Osteen concerning the supreme consideration of all religions. Specifically, who *is* Jesus, and is He truly the *only* way to heaven? Pastor Osteen needed only a top hat and cane as he danced all around the issue. Larry King pressed further:

> King: "But you believe your way?"
>
> Osteen: "I believe my way. I believe my way with all my heart."
>
> King: "But for someone who doesn't share it is wrong, isn't he?"
>
> Osteen: "Well, yes. Well, I don't know if I look at it like that. I would present my way, but I'm just going to let God be the judge of that. I don't know. I don't know."
>
> King: "So you make no judgment on anyone?"

Osteen: "No. But I..."

King: "What about atheists?"

Osteen: "You know what? I'm going to let someone...I'm going to let God be the judge of who
goes to heaven and hell. I just...again, I present
the truth, and I say it every week. You know, I
believe it's a relationship with Jesus. But you know
what? I'm not going to go around telling everybody
else if they don't want to believe that that's going
to be their choice. God's got to look at your own
heart. God's got to look at your heart, and only
God knows that."[25]

If Pastor Osteen indeed presents the gospel truth every
week as he stated, I have yet to hear it in the many times
I have listened to his broadcast over the past four years.

The popularity of the prosperity message, laced
with partial truths and sprinkled with Scripture (usually
devoid of context), is nevertheless the kind of message we
want to be true. Sadly, the desire of one's heart, enticed
by the ringing of what one longs to hear, has eclipsed the
balanced truth of the great news of Christ crucified and
risen from the grave. With biblical knowledge already
woefully low, both inside and outside the church, (see
previous chapters) and exegetical rigors forgotten or forsaken by many of today's pastors, the path to physical
and financial success is enthusiastically embraced.

His best-selling book, *Your Best Life Now*, begins
with Pastor Osteen recounting a story of a man and his
wife vacationing in Hawaii.[26] Taken with the beauty of
the islands, they pass a home that is situated on a high
point overlooking the Pacific and all its spectacular grandeur of tropical paradise. The man wistfully exclaims, "I

can't even imagine living in a place like that." But there's a voice in his head that says, *Don't worry. You won't. You will never live in a great place like that.* The man is surprised at his own thoughts, and he inquires as to his own thinking. "As long as you can't imagine it, as long as you can't see it, then it is not going to happen for you."[27]

Osteen gets to the punch line of the story.

> The man correctly realized that his own thoughts and attitudes were condemning him to mediocrity. He determined then and there to start believing better of himself and believing better of God. It's the same with us.

Osteen continues, "We have to conceive it on the inside before we're ever going to receive it on the outside."

I acknowledge it is easy to take a cheap shot at someone, especially when they cannot respond. I have been mindful as I proceed that it is just as unfair to take isolated snippets from Pastor Osteen's book, using convenient excerpts to prove points, as it is using the Bible in the same way. Therefore, I have truly tried to be even-handed in my dealing with such excerpts, and I have tried also to extend the benefit of doubt at every instance.

In my estimation, I am fairly representing what Pastor Osteen and the rest of his kind are teaching. In fact, the more you read of *Your Best Life Now*, the more strained it becomes, not better. Admittedly, toward the end of his book, Osteen actually stumbles—in spite of himself it seems—onto some bona fide biblical principles that ironically head butt much of what precedes them. The apparent contradictions, though, pose no problems for Osteen or the millions who hang on his words. This is unfortunate yet a potent sign of the times.

As I have mentioned, error is rarely apprehended with enthusiasm if it is presented in all its erroneous unsightliness. Today's peddlers of prosperity are exquisitely proficient at gift wrapping when it comes to repackaging error with bright, pleasant paper, meticulously crafted bows of flowing ribbon, and a glittering of truth.

Turn-of-the-century Anglican Bishop J. C. Ryle explains the truth of this allure in *A Call to Holiness*:

> Temptation to sin will rarely present itself to us in its true colours saying, "I am your deadly enemy, and I want to ruin you forever in hell." Oh no! Sin comes to us like Judas, with a kiss; like Joab, with an out stretched hand and flattering words.[28]

The appeal of the prosperity message is its attractiveness to our baser selves. And yet the similarities of some of the hallmarks of the prosperity message to an earlier epoch are worthy of comment.

13

THERE REALLY IS NOTHING NEW

If Mary Baker Eddy, the founder of Christian Science, was the progenitor of the prosperity mindset in 1866, it realized a secularized repackaging about a hundred years later. The New Age movement was going full bore around the time I was entering pastoral ministry. Shirley MacLaine became "Surely Acclaimed" with her New Age autobiographical book, *Out on a Limb*, though even by Hollywood's standards, she was a bit of a laughingstock. Ruth Montgomery, one of the matriarchs of the movement, taught her devotees about the *Strangers Among Us*. Montgomery's "walk-ins" were spirit beings who, if given entrance, would occupy a person, giving them spiritual insight, wisdom, enlightenment, and clairvoyant powers. Also, one of the rising stars of the celestial children was Peruvian-born, American writer Carlos Casteneda, the essential patriarch of the movement. Casteneda, with his own little New Age spin, touted an Americanized shamanism replete with powers to heal and the rest.

The gurus of the New Age all had their own little niche, for the most part, but the one common element in the New Age faith was the power inherent to every individual to "create one's own reality." Through a process called visualization, one was able to tap into their "divine spark" and, through thinking the right thoughts, could actually create or change the reality around them. The anecdotal evidence for the validity of the power of New Age visualization is not much different than many of the testimonies one hears now from the adherents of the prosperity message. Solomon wrote, "There is nothing new under the sun," and there is certainly nothing new about "creating one's own reality."

The power of the mind *is* strong. Medical science has documented many cases of people dying of various maladies because they thought they were dying of various maladies. In fact, objective medical analysis revealed they were not diseased at all. Likewise, it has been documented that some people have been healed of serious diseases when given a placebo because they thought the placebo was some new, highly effective medicine. There is a legitimate aspect to mind over matter, but even that is not necessarily consistent, and it certainly isn't divine. While not everyone who practiced or attempted New Age visualization was tapping into another realm, there can be a thin line between naïve mind games and an intrusion by spirits.

I have written earlier that as a teenager, I returned to the Christian Science church with my parents. The mind games of Mary Baker Eddy and the power of positive thinking (in the vernacular of Christian Science, it is called holding good thoughts) are at the very foundation of Christian Science. Mrs. Eddy writes:

> After lengthy examination of my discovery and its demonstration in healing the sick, this fact became evident to me—that Mind governs the body not partially but wholly.[29]

Two pages later, she continues:

> Christian Science explains all cause and effect as mental not physical…It shows the scientific relation of man to God, disentangles the interlaced ambiguities of being and sets free the imprisoned thought.[30]

When I was a teenager, I was working as a janitor at a Skil Power tools factory in suburban Chicago. One evening, I was pulling two wheeled containers that were made from steel into which I would throw the cardboard and refuse I gathered from around the plant floor. These carts were about eight feet in length and four feet in width, weighing, I would guess, a couple hundred pounds apiece when empty. As I was pulling one behind me and pushing another in front of me, the front container stopped fast, as one of its wheels jammed on a screw on the floor. The screw, acting like a wedge, stopped the cart almost instantly. However, the trailing cart continued and caught my heel as I was stepping, tearing the flesh down the back of my foot. It wasn't a serious injury, but it was bleeding.

Being the novice Christian Scientist, I applied the mental gymnastics I had learned concerning my being a perfect creation of God, that matter is unreal, that material being is a product of mortal mind. Consequently, pain and physical imperfection are merely the result of wrong thinking. And yes, there are even scriptures tacked on to the whole bizarre Christian Science mess. As I continued with my work, I recited out loud:

> Behold, what manner of love the Father hath bestowed upon us, that we should be called the sons of God: therefore the world knoweth us not, because it knew him not. Beloved, now are we the sons of God, and it doth not yet appear what we shall be: but we know that, when he shall appear, we shall be like him; for we shall see him as he is.
>
> 1 John 3:1–2 (KJV)

The application of the passage to my situation hung on the snippet of scripture that says, "We shall be like him." In the parlance of Christian Science mumbo jumbo, it meant that I am just like Jesus and He wouldn't be bothered by such a physical annoyance. After all, He was the great physician and would heal himself. Therefore, I had the power to heal myself just like Him.

I looked down at my heel, realizing that it did not hurt any longer, but what took even me aback was that the skin which had clearly been scraped away by the steal cart and the blood were all gone. There was no trace that I had ever hurt my heel. What to make of it…

Years later, when I came to the place of renouncing Christian Science as the religion that is neither Christian nor scientific, my perspective on what happened that day became clear. My healing, which was genuine, occurred by the power of the devil for the purpose of pulling me deeper into the false religion of Mary Baker Eddy. This is no quick or harsh judgment about the religion but is the result of careful study of *Science and Health* against the truth of the Bible. Mrs. Eddy writes:

> Wisdom and Love may require many sacrifices of self to save us from sin. One sacrifice, however great, is insufficient to pay the debt of sin. The atonement requires constant self-immolation on the sinner's part. That God's wrath should be vented upon his own beloved Son is divinely unnatural. Such a theory is manmade.[31]

Even in my spiritual infancy, I knew enough of the Bible to know that Mrs. Eddy just jettisoned the very means of my hope of salvation. Satan, I believe, was trying to pull me away for my sincere quest for truth, which he is capable of doing. This is why Paul warns the Corinthians, "Even Satan disguises himself as an angel of light" (2 Corinthians 11:14). Paul is speaking about false teachers who appear to be good people, who appear to say some really nice things, even lacing their speech with plenty of god talk.

Do not misunderstand. I do not believe that Pastor Osteen or the other prosperity peddlers are cult leaders or are intending to teach shamanic mind games, New Age visualization, or Christian Science methodology. But at the end of the day, there is little difference in the foundations upon which the New Age message and the prosperity message are erected. Pastor Osteen at least makes frequent reference to a personal God, whereas the New Age movement was all about an impersonal divine force. Still, it is inescapable that *Your Best Life Now* is a classic presentation of the prosperity gospel teaching you how to obtain what *you* want when *you* want it. Your only limitation is *your* faith in *your* ability to believe and to think opportunities, circumstances, and "blessing" into existence.

After explaining that your life blessings (i.e., prosperity) will follow your expectations, Osteen writes, "What you expect is what you will get."[32]

What you expect is what you'll get? Really? Does anyone ever ask, "Is this *true?*"

I would answer that whole tenor of life as it unravels is so blatantly against the truthfulness of the prosperity paradigm that you wouldn't think asking would be necessary. It is demonstrably false at nearly every turn. I don't know what your life is like or what your thought processes are like, but if what Pastor Osteen asserts is true, we wouldn't have what I call the *American Idol* syndrome today.

Prosperity and the American Idol Syndrome

If Osteen is right and "you get what you expect," we wouldn't have what I call the *American Idol* syndrome. Each season, tens of thousands of aspiring musicians wend their way through the maze of reviews and critiques, being eliminated one by one, facing a new round of judgment. By the time we see the remaining handful on television, the truly untalented have been weeded out, except for those (I assume) who are deemed to have some entertainment value for the viewing public. But what is obvious season after season is that there are many, many people who have truly put their heart and soul, time, and money into their dreams of being the next American

Idol. There is no lack of expectation in these wannabe stars; there is no paucity of passion, no scarcity of sincerity. If "what you expect is what you will get," there would be many more millionaires in this country and more professional athletes on every sports team in the world than all of sports could accommodate. Talent-laden pop stars would be a dime a dozen.

What is particularly revealing on *American Idol* is the contestants who are reduced to sobbing, tears, or outrage when they are told not only that they aren't good enough to advance in the competition but that they need to think of doing something else with their lives altogether.

Sometimes blood, sweat, and tears; fervent, heartfelt desire; great expectation; and even ceaseless hard work are no guarantee of a prosperous future.

And fortunately, it works in reverse as well with success, sometimes being conferred on someone in spite of their mental frame of mind, confidence, desire, or expectation.

When I was in grammar school, I joined the YMCA in town. What I didn't know was that, in joining, I had also volunteered to be a part of any fund-raising efforts on behalf of the organization. It was time for the annual YMCA cookie sale, and we were each given a case of cookies with which to begin canvassing our neighborhoods. Unfortunately, the cookie drive always came in the middle of winter. My cardboard case had a pop-up cardboard handle, and inside, it contained twelve boxes of cookies. It was the size of a three-suiter luggage case and felt like (and looked like) I was toting anvils from door to door.

Being diminutive for my age, I struggled to keep the case off the snow-covered sidewalks I would traverse after mustering up the nerve to bang on a door. I *hated* knocking on doors, trying to sell my wares; I hated the freezing winds fighting against my pedestrian efforts with my cardboard anchor acting as a ship's mast, never in my favor. A natural salesman I wasn't, and my pitch was the same at every house: "You don't want to buy any of these cookies, do ya?" My teeth were usually chattering, lips purple, my torso barely visible behind my cardboard refuge. To my shock, I sold my case out and had to obtain another case from the Y. At the end of the fund drive, I had sold more cookies than all but two other kids.

If it is true that you get what you expect, I would have returned the first case, un-entered by human hands, except for the two boxes my parents obligingly purchased.

If you're protesting, "Joel isn't talking about cookies!" No, he isn't per se, but whether you're talking about baked dough or painted sheet rock, it's merely a difference in degree. Let's take a more appropriate anecdote that mitigates Pastor Osteen's thesis of, you get what you expect.

In 1990, I began writing an op-ed column for the central Maine newspapers. Before moving to Maine, I had a written a few guest (religion) columns for a suburban Chicago newspaper. So when I came to town in Waterville, Maine, I figured I would shoot a sample of my previous articles over to the editor of the central Maine newspapers to see if they would have any interest in my writing a column for them. I explained that while I didn't really want to write a religion column per se, I would certainly be writing from a Christian worldview.

I knew the odds of them wanting to take me up on my offer were slim. After all, I was a right-wing conservative, Bible-believing pastor new to the area with little experience, and the paper had a pointedly liberal bend to it. I fully expected to get rejected but figured nothing ventured, nothing gained.

So when I received a phone call from one of the editors who said he liked my idea, I was stunned. He said they couldn't pay me much, but, again, I was stunned. I expected to write simply for the opportunity; I saw it could be engaging the secular mind with the truth of God's Word. To be paid and to be right on the op-ed page opposite the liberal editorial of the paper's staff was unbelievable. Obviously, I didn't get what I expected. But God had plans for me in spite of my aspirations, my lack of expectation, and my lack of faith.

A few months into my writing for the paper, one of the editors informed me of a contest they were aware of that was open to Christians who were writing for the secular press. They gave me the information, and all I had to do was submit a published article that met their criteria. Once again, there was nothing required on my part but to send them something. So for the cost of a postage stamp, there was the possibility that I could win $1,000, not to mention the prestige of the award itself.

As I looked into the details of the contest annually sponsored by the Amy Foundation, I saw that Cal Thomas, Michael Medved, Charles Colson, and a host of who's who in Christendom had been past award winners. In all honesty, my expectations were zilch.

Several months later, when I was notified that I was a finalist my first time entering, I was pleased but didn't understand what that meant. As I continued to read the letter, as a finalist, I was guaranteed at least one of the awards of merit, which was $1,000. I was simply dumbfounded. I read and reread the letter, certain I must have misunderstood it, but when another envelope arrived with congratulations and check for a cool grand, I was a believer. As it turned out, I would go on to win three more $1,000 awards in my nine years of writing for the *Central Maine Morning Sentinel* and the *Kennebec Journal*. That was not at all what I expected.

Pastor Osteen, in his fervent desire to see people wearing smiles again (a good trait to be sure), writes:

> You too may have assumed that you've already peaked, that you've reached your limits in life, that you will never be more successful. I'll never achieve significance, do something meaningful or enjoy the good things in life that I've seen others enjoy. Sad to say, you are exactly right…unless you are willing to change your thinking. That's why the first step to living at your full potential is to enlarge your vision.[33]

Osteen then continues with what edges closer to the shamanic mind games of the New Age than living biblical truth.

> To live your best life now, you must start looking at life through eyes of faith, seeing yourself rising to new levels. See your business taking off. See your marriage restored. See your family prospering. See your dreams coming to pass. You must conceive it and believe it is possible if you ever hope to experience it.[34]

14

THE PROSPERITY GOSPEL NEEDS PROPER EXEGESIS

In true character to the broader panorama of prosperity poppycock, sound exegesis[3] of the Scriptures rarely, if ever, comes into play. Right from the beginning of *Your Best Life Now*, you are introduced to the level of scholarship in dividing the Word of God that will carry throughout Pastor Osteen's writing.

All the prosperity preachers I have heard and read pull out their favorite passages, which, when taken in isolation of the rest of Scripture, seem to endorse their strained view of things. They all tend to have the same basic arsenal of prepackaged verses they resort to when they need a spiritual sounding gloss to sanctify their pitch.

---

[3] Exegesis is the proper procedure for pulling out of the Scripture what is actually there, what the author intended to mean. Eisogesis, the opposite, is the procedure of infusing into Scripture what you want it to mean to suit your purposes.

One such passage that is a favorite of the prosperity peddlers is John 10:10: "I have come to give you life more abundant." This becomes their springboard for diving into the pool of spiritual fantasy and lavish "blessings" of material wonder. It is *prima facie* evidence that the good news apparently the rest of us are missing is the good news of riches, success, health, fame, and whatever else we determine to be vital to our happiness in this life now. They insist this is why Jesus came according to John 10:10.

But the rest of the passage from which verse 10 is extracted is not about material prosperity primarily or even secondarily but is about the real meaning of and obtainment of eternal life.

> Truly, truly, I say to you, he who does not enter by the door into the fold of the sheep, but climbs up some other way, he is a thief and a robber…
>
> John 10:1

Instead of us assuming what Jesus meant—or worse, infusing what Jesus said with what we might want Him to say—the Bible interprets the Bible for us. Additionally, the Bible is also forthright. It even tells us when the people listening firsthand, who should have understood what Jesus meant, didn't. And the Bible even lets us know when something is to be taken figuratively. Almost in editorial fashion, for our benefit, the Holy Spirit notes: "This figure of speech Jesus spoke to them, but they did not understand what those things were which He had been saying to them" (John 10:6).

So Jesus gives it another shot. He doesn't want them to misunderstand. (Take note. If you are in a position of leadership and you get flummoxed that the people you are teaching don't get it, be encouraged. Sometimes when our omniscient, omni-talented, omni-gifted Savior spoke, people stood looking at Him like cows staring at a new gate.)

> So Jesus said to them again, "Truly, truly, I say to you, I am the door of the sheep. All who came before Me are thieves and robbers, but the sheep did not hear them. I am the door; if anyone enters through Me, he will be saved, and will go in and out and find pasture."
>
> John 10:7

In context, Jesus is explaining metaphorically (the passage tells us that), using a sheepfold, that there is only *one* way to heaven and that is through the One entrance, which happens to be a person—the person of Jesus. "Truly, truly, I say to you, he who does not enter by the door into the fold of the sheep, but climbs up some other way, he is a thief and a robber" (John 10:1).

So the important backdrop (context) against which the so-called "abundant life" verse is situated is that there is only One way to enter into this eternal life, even though there are many who will try to entice someone with other avenues. Jesus calls such people thieves and robbers who come "only to steal and destroy." It is at this point that Jesus utters the words highjacked by the purveyors of prosperity: "I came that they may have life, and have it abundantly" (John 10:10).

The passage is first and foremost about eternal life. Eternal life is comprehensive. Yes, *eternal* means forever, certainly, but the very nature of the eternal ultimately makes any reference to time irrelevant. To speak of eternity past or eternity future is nonsensical. Eternity just is. It is the always now, the ever-present.

When Jesus said, "Before Abraham was, I AM," in John 8:58, He was indicating that He was indeed God Almighty, the One without beginning, without middle, and without end. He is I AM. And our eternal God's fervent passion and reason for coming to earth at all was to secure eternal life for all who would receive it.

And for we who are mortals, who did come into being, who are, in fact, time-bound, the promise of eternal life commences the moment we receive Christ. In other words (at the risk of sounding self-contradicting), eternal life *begins,* for the Christian, the moment he receives salvation. So when we think of eternal life, we must prohibit our minds from picturing something that "starts" only after we die and have gone to heaven.

When Jesus becomes one's Savior, eternal life begins then and there, and the relationship that was breached between that one and God because of sin has been resolved. Our favored status before God the Father is forever changed. We who were once sin filled and condemned are now, in Christ, credited with the very sinlessness of Jesus Himself. God is forever and always on our side. All His favor that we could ever receive was given to us the moment we believe. We will never have any *more* favor than the favor of being clothed with the perfection of Jesus (Isaiah 61:10).

This is precisely why the Christian's eternal life is as secure and "abundant" as Jesus Himself. Eternal life then *is* the abundant life, for nothing surpasses a new relationship with God as your friend. God Himself said,

"I will never leave you nor forsake you!" (Hebrews 13:5). Is it fair to say that the companionship of God Almighty surpasses anything and everything else this world has to offer, including a dream home or star power?

What should be eye-opening to the prosperites and their mentors is that this promise of God's companionship through thick and thin is also in an interesting context. Without that context, even the verse I intentionally only partially cited is merely another proof text, and proof texts can easily mislead. What a different passage it becomes when read as intended.

> Make sure that your character is free from the love of money, being content with what you have; *for* He Himself has said, "I will never desert you, nor will I ever forsake you..." *so that* we confidently say, "The Lord is my helper, I will not be afraid. What will man do to me?"
>
> Hebrews 13:5–6

Rather than a *carte blanche* to presumptuously invoke God's favor at my beck and call, like a cosmic bellhop, the promise above is conditioned on my properly aligning my priorities with God's priorities. Instead of enlarging my vision, telling God (for example) that I *see* my book published, that I *believe* it *will* be published, and that I *expect* it will be wildly successful so that I will be able to upgrade to a nicer house with a better view, the biblical perspective is that I need to learn to be truly content with what I have (Hebrews 13:5). I need truly to be content with who I am because the King of the universe is my closest friend. That is far greater than anything and everything else this place of temporary habitation can offer. What a far cry this is from the prosperity preacher's "Name it; claim it! See it; believe it, because you *deserve* it." The truth is we do *not* always get what we deserve. Thank God.

Jesus's assuring His followers that He came to give "life abundant" is no promise of a trouble-free life, a life of material grandeur, or a life free from pain and suffering, as the prosperity peddlers sell. Rather, it is a promise that no matter what we go through in this life, even a life of turmoil and pain, we can expect the companionship of God Himself. And because of His presence with us, we can experience abundance of life in spite of the circumstances rather than because of them.

Paul tells the believers at Rome that God alone can and will take all the nastiness of this life and shape that nastiness "together for good" (as defined by God) and it will be glorious. This is what it means to have the abundant life, and when one is experiencing *this* kind of abundant life, one truly experiences their best life now.

As I write this, a dear fifty-something friend of mine has been informed that her ovarian cancer is back. It had been in remission for three years since her surgery. She and her husband were reeled, as all her tests had shown that she was cancer free. But after getting over the initial shock, one evening, she was telling us what happened only a few days later.

> Three years ago, lying in the hospital bed after major surgery, my surgeon/oncologist came to speak to me. He told me that I have almost stage three ovarian cancer. Not only was it an aggressive cancer but very rare as well. As he was telling me all this, I had a vision in my mind/heart of

the overwhelming love God had for me, that I was important in His eyes, that He wanted me to fill a job that no one else could do for Him. Just as He assigned Jesus, His perfect Son, to wear a crown of thorns, He wanted me to carry cancer.

This vision of Christ wearing the crown of thorns was a vision I had many times while going through the grueling rounds of chemo. If Christ could endure the thorns and take the nails, then I, by golly, was going to take the chemo with some grace, dignity, and much gratitude.

Now, three years later, I have been told the cancer not only returned but now I will live with it while being treated for it the rest of my life. That is not what I wanted to hear, but it is a cross I am no less willing to bear, if that is what God wants. I truly feel this way because God, so many times before, showed Himself to me as an up close and very personal God during the last cancer. I knew I could trust Him to be with me and give me exactly what I needed when I needed it, and I needed faith.

After the shocking news that my cancer had returned, I was back in church. No one knew the news I was carrying. A sweet couple came up to me with a gift bag in hand. The woman said to me that what was in the bag was very special to her and her husband. As they were praying to the Lord about whom to give this gift to, my name came to them.

While holding the unopened gift, I was telling a friend how the cancer had returned. Through tears, we held each other, and my friend said, "Why does this have to be? How are you going to get though this?" I responded by telling her of my ongoing vision of the crown of thrones, and that's how I will get through anything. We said our good-byes and went into service.

When I got home from church, I opened my gift. My breath was taken away as I sat down and cried and cried. The gift was a beautiful drawing of crown of thorns, and sitting in the middle of the crown was a lamb.

This couple had no idea about my story and the significance that this picture would hold for me. They just did as they were lead to do through prayer. For me, it was clear that God was saying, "I'm still here, and I still need you," but, more importantly, "*I love you.*"

Wow. God loves me enough that He even gave me a physical picture to show it. That picture hangs at the foot of my bed. It is the first thing I see each morning and the last thing I see as the lights go out.

Remember the prosperity preacher's teaching about sickness that I mentioned?

It's never God's will for us to be sick; He wants every person healed every time. That's nearly-too-good-to-be-true news, but that's the gospel.[35]

When you see the hideous visage of the prosperity message juxtaposed to the beauty of the abundant life of one of God's precious lambs, it makes me seethe with anger. When Jesus was explaining the difference between the real shepherd and his love for his sheep versus the posers, the imposters, the ne'er-do-wells who pretend to have the interests of the sheep at heart, He tells it like it is. "The thief comes only to steal and kill and destroy..."

Can you imagine how many men and women who sincerely love the Lord are crushed by despair, having fallen prey to the pilferers of "real" prosperity? Buying the twisted prosperity of the scammers, they wonder why they haven't been healed of their sickness, or, worse, they blame themselves for not conjuring up enough faith, not believing hard enough, not enlarging their vision broad enough.

My friend's cancer is an insult, to be sure—the product of living in a fallen world where the consequences of sin still rule over Satan's domain. Bad things *do* happen to good people; the rain does fall on the just and the unjust alike. We easily forget that this planet is not the kingdom of God and this is *not* our home. "We are aliens and exiles," according to Paul, but most of us have driven our tent stakes deep into the soil of this world, and the infectious prosperity gospel encourages, fosters, and demands as much.

Unlike the gospel of prosperity, the gospel of Jesus takes something as hideous as ovarian cancer and turns it from something ugly, defeating, and pointless into something that is a glory to God.

My friend and her husband have their down moments. They are still human, still living in bodies of flesh that are waiting to be renewed beyond corruptibility. But as my friend walks through the valley of the shadow of death with the joy of a Risen Savior at her side, it is a joy that surpasses the circumstances and yields a peace that is beyond understanding. *This* is the abundant life of which Jesus spoke. And as she and her husband traverse this path, many are being touched by her allowing herself to be used by the One who purchased her body, soul, and spirit with His very own blood.

Certainly, there will be times of weeping as we all walk with her and her husband and her children through this insult of living in a fallen world. But thanks be to God, there is something better around the corner. And that "something better" is the same "something better" that God said He had in store for all the believers who suffered terribly for their love of God in faith's hall of fame in the book of Hebrews.

In the midst of the crucible of life, God's people are living through the searing flames of trial because the Good Shepherd promised, "I came that they may have life, and have it abundantly" (John 10:10).

"Peace I leave with you; My peace I give to you; not as the world gives do I give to you. Do not let your heart be troubled, nor let it be fearful" (John 14:27).

If only there was a disciplined commitment to the inspired, infallible, inerrant, authoritative Word of God. Needless to say, there is a dearth of attention to well grounded exegesis in the prosperity panoply.

15

THE PROSPERITY PEDDLERS TORTURE THE INSPIRED TEXT

It is Wednesday morning, and I am painfully enduring Danette Crawford, hostess of the program called *Joy in the Morning*.[36] The attractive woman comes on and exuberantly proclaims, "It is turnaround time!" alluding to a turnaround of whatever it is from which her listeners would like to be turned around.

"I need my miracle today!" she says with a smile.

She jumps into a moment of prayer, directing viewers to put one hand on the afflicted part of their body, and commands them to extend the other hand toward their TV screen while she begins to pray for them. As she is praying, she says she feels the anointing of the Holy Spirit. She finishes praying and makes fleeting mention of her ministry and preaching the Word of God, but she hasn't mentioned anything from the Bible at all. Then finally, she goes to her teaching, which, after hearing it, would have been better if she had skipped it altogether.

"I'm in Galatians four, four through five," she says.

I don't recall if she read both verses or only a piece of them. It didn't matter either way, since what the text says and the way she used it bear no resemblance.

Here is what the passage actually says: "But when the fullness of the time came, God sent forth His Son, born of a woman, born under the Law, so that He might redeem those who were under the Law, that we might receive the adoption as sons" (Galatians 4:4–5).

In these profound verses, Paul explains the significance of the incarnation using an illustration of a child who is an heir to a great estate, but when the heir is just a child, he is still under the authority of those over him. Using familiar language of a family situation where there has been an adoption, the passage speaks of our inheritance in Jesus, as well as whom the believer is in Christ. In a creative manipulation of the inspired text, Ms. Crawford uses it to note that God's timing is always right, so "you need to just hang on to your miracle because the job is coming, the money is coming, and God is going to bless you financially." I said out loud, "Huh?" She jumps over to John 7:8, which says, "Go up to the feast yourselves. I do not go up to this feast because My time has not yet fully come."

In the context of John 7, Jesus is instructing his brothers to go on ahead to the feast in Judea but informs them that He was staying back in Galilee. In another creative twist of the Scripture, this priestess of prosperity uses the passage to tell the viewers they have to "wait for their miracle."

Finally, in what is such an obtuse use of Scripture that I have a hard time writing it, she cites Isaiah 49:7, which says:

> Thus says the LORD, the Redeemer of Israel and
> its Holy One, To the despised One, To the One
> abhorred by the nation, To the Servant of rulers,
> "Kings will see and arise, Princes will also bow
> down, Because of the LORD who is faithful, the
> Holy One of Israel who has chosen You."

This beautiful, prophetic word is about the rejection of the coming Messiah upon his first advent but then brings in the eventual acknowledgement of his Lordship at His second advent.

Ms. Crawford's paraphrase of the passage concluded with something about, "While you're waiting for your turnaround, remember God has been faithful."

With my mind faltering, I am not exactly sure what she said, as I was about to lose consciousness from such a dizzying handling of God's Word. She cruised through all three of these complex passages in less than five minutes, and it might have been more like two. Typically, this kind of non-exegesis is a given when it comes to the peddlers of prosperity.

In *Your Best Life Now*, Pastor Osteen takes the story of the wineskins recorded in Matthew, Mark, and Luke, conveniently using it to illustrate what he views as the scriptural validation of his "new" paradigm. He calls it the need for us to "enlarge our vision of life." Osteen writes, "Interestingly, when Jesus wanted to encourage His followers to enlarge their visions, He reminded them, 'You can't put new wine into old wineskins.' Jesus was saying that you cannot have a larger life with restricted attitudes. The lesson is still relevant today."[37]

In the situation to which Jesus responded, Jesus was dealing with the hypocritical Pharisees of the day who had no interest in the truth. Their questions were not born out of a sincere desire to know what is right, but they only wanted to catch Jesus with something for which they could accuse Him and get rid of Him once and for all. This is a far cry from it being a lesson in expanding your desire for a greater income, a nicer house, a better title, or fame.

But the abuse of Scripture increases as you go deeper into this superficial treatment of what is nothing more than self-absorbed greed. Pastor Osteen gives us his interpretive spin concerning Elijah and his servant, Elisha. He writes:

> The career of the Old Testament prophet Elijah offers some fascinating insights. Elijah experienced numerous miracles and his understudy, Elisha, witnessed many of them. As Elijah neared the end of his life, he asked Elisha what he would like to have from his mentor. "I want a double portion of your spirit," Elisha replied boldly.[38]

Osteen then recounts Elijah's reply to Elisha about seeing Elijah being taken up in the whirlwind. Osteen explains its meaning:

> Certainly in a literal sense Elijah was telling Elisha, "If God allows you to see it, you can count on your request being granted." But we can't help but wonder if Elijah was also saying, "If you can see it you can be it. If you can visualize it in your heart and mind, seeing it through the screen of God's Word with your 'spiritual eyes,' it can become a reality in your life."[39]

These brief examples—samples really—of what inundates the prosperity message grow increasingly more egregious to anyone interested in biblical theology. Pastor Osteen asserts, "The fourth aspect—and one of the most important—to developing a fresh vision for your life is discovering how to experience more of God's favor."[40]

More of God's favor? When Jesus came to this earth to live for me, the Father declared, "This is my Son in whom I am well pleased" (Matthew 3:17). When Jesus went to Calvary to die for me, the Father was pleased to pour out His anger toward my sin upon the One who was sinless. When my precious Jesus rose from the grave, defeating physical and spiritual death once for all who believe, God showed His favor on me to the nth degree. Every morning that I awake and put my feet on the floor, I experience God's favor to the full because of all that I have been declared to be by God in Christ, not by my positive thinking, not by visualizing my dreams, not by "seeing it, believing it, expecting it," but by the magnanimous, unilateral act of God's love in sending His Son, our Savior.

The interpretive foolishness grows more foolish, as Osteen writes:

> The Bible clearly states, "God has crowned us with glory and honor…" In other words, God wants to make your life easier. He wants to assist you, to promote you, to give you advantages. He wants you to have preferential treatment. But if we're going to experience more of God's favor we must live more "favor-minded." To be favor-minded means that

we expect God's special help, and we are releasing our faith, knowing that God wants to assist us.[41]

I am not sure how Jesus gets pushed out of consideration and evaluation of Pastor Osteen's advice, but his advice bears little resemblance to the counsel of God's Word from the Apostle Paul.

> Do nothing from selfishness or empty conceit, but with humility of mind regard one another as more important than yourselves; do not merely look out for your own personal interests, but also for the interests of others. Have this attitude in yourselves which was also in Christ Jesus, who, although He existed in the form of God, did not regard equality with God a thing to be grasped, but emptied Himself, taking the form of a bond-servant, and being made in the likeness of men. Being found in appearance as a man, He humbled Himself by becoming obedient to the point of death, even death on a cross.
>
> Philippians 2:3–8

One more example (though there are many others) is warranted concerning this prosperity preacher's avoidance of the exegetical method in explaining and applying the infallible Word of God.

Pastor Osteen recalls the story of Sarah and Abraham and the glorious promise God made to Abraham all the way back in Genesis 12:1–3. In theology, it is called the Proto-evangelium. It means the "first gospel," the first revelation of God's spectacular plan for the redemption of mankind. As Abraham and Sarah age, the plan is fleshed out in bits and pieces by God's revealing of his plan for a child to be born to Abraham and Sarah. Osteen recounts how Abraham and Sarah tried to help God out by impregnating Abraham's concubine Hagar, since the promise of a child wasn't happening fast enough for their liking. Osteen, yet again, manipulated by his obsession with the power of positive thinking in creating or bringing about one's desired reality, writes the following:

> Still more years went by, and no child. Finally, Sarah became pregnant. What changed? God's promise was the same all along. I'm convinced that the key to the promise coming to pass was that Sarah had to conceive it in her heart before she was able to conceive it in her physical body. She had to believe she could become pregnant before she actually became with child.[42]

In the land of the prosperity gospel, God's plans for an individual, as well as mankind, is not dependent on God as much as on some frivolous exercise in mind over matter. This profound lack of biblical exegesis is disturbing, as are the positive pastor's examples from his own life that he uses to punctuate his points.

Pastor Osteen relates an incident when he was pulled over by a policeman for speeding. Joel's father was pastor at the time. After Osteen handed the officer his license, the officer just stared at it and then said:

> "Are you related to that ahh...that ahhh, that preacher?" By the way he spit out the words I didn't know whether it was going to be a good thing to be related to Daddy. And I don't know why I answered him this way, but I think it was because I was nervous. I smiled and said, "Well Officer, it

all depends." He glared at me and said, "Boy what are you talking about?" I said, "It all depends on whether you like him or not." He looked up in the air a real long time. At least a long enough for me to think, "Hmmm, that's not a good sign, if he has to think about it." Then he looked back at me, cracked a hint of a smile and said, "Yes I like him a lot." "Good" I said. "Because that's my dad, and I'm sure he wouldn't want you to give me a ticket." Believe it or not, the officer let me go.[43]

Then Pastor Osteen concludes his life example, writing: "The point is, of course, that I received preferential treatment, not because of me, but because of my father."[44]

On its own two feet, the illustration is well placed and clarifies his meaning in an entertaining way. But it also illustrates what Pastor Osteen teaches—perhaps unintentionally—over and over, and that is that God is there to be used for our benefit, our advantage, and our preferential treatment.

What is ironic about the pastor's illustration about speeding and the demand of preferential treatment is what he later writes on page 164, in his chapter ironically titled, "Let God Bring Justice into Your Life": "God has promised if we will put our trust in Him, He will pay us back for all the unfair things that have happened to us."[45]

This is strained at best. While it is true—ultimately—such justice is not guaranteed in this lifetime, and frankly, that's not always desirable at any rate.

If Pastor Osteen received justice when he was pulled over for speeding, he would have been paying a fine or worse. What Osteen really means is that when injustice works to your favor, it's not unjust; it's preferential treatment. Otherwise, everyone should demand their rights as a child of the King who deserves preferential treatment. But preferential treatment by definition implies, by its very nature, that someone else will receive less than what they deserve, which will be unjust. The logic of the prosperity message is dizzying.

Many years ago, my wife and I had some friends over ushering in the New Year by watching a six-hour video series called the *Holiness of God* by R. C. Sproul. At one point, Dr. Sproul explained what we all truly deserve because of our sin. Then he said, "Don't ever demand justice. You just might get it."

If God had given us justice, every one of us would be bound for hell.

16

THE SINKING SAND
OF PROSPERITY

Whether turning on the television to watch the purveyors of a more prosperous life, reading their offerings
online, or suffering through a bestseller, the only ones
who seem to be truly prospering are the peddlers themselves. They have their lineup of "testimonies" extolling
the "miraculous" results of what happened when they
spent money on the book, made a contribution to the
ministry, or sent in their seed faith pledge. I have no
doubt that some—maybe even many—have had some
noteworthy results. But as I was reading some of the
stories in *Your Best Life Now*, I remembered the latter portion of *Science and Health*. In the chapter called
"Fruitage," Mrs. Eddy has included page after page of
people of who were miraculously healed through the
application of Christian Science. But as I already noted
from my own pilgrimage in this religion of blasphemous
and bizarre beliefs, I too experienced miraculous healing
but also noted that it was not from God.

Even if some people do experience extraordinary
results from the prosperity preachers' instruction, do the

ends to anything always or ever justify the means? Let's for a moment say that the peddlers of prosperity are doing a service for the masses who would otherwise be depressed or at least stuck or complacent with the status quo of their routine. Is there any harm in giving people hope, even if it might be a bit overstated or simplistic?

I would suggest that if we were discussing a different issue, say, a doctor talking to a terminal patient, and he painted the brightest possible picture of the future that he could, unless he was utterly lying, we might excuse his good intention. We might even call it compassion. But we are not talking about a purely human endeavor, such as medicine, where there are obvious limits to what a doctor can know for certain about his patient and their prognosis. Such is not the case with the revelation of God concerning our past, present, and future. The Bible was given as a manual for life, and in it, we are given many God-ordered principles that govern our lives. But even in those patterns for life, there is a much greater theme, and it isn't learning how to invest ourselves, our time, and our resources in pursuit of heaven on Earth.

The grand theme that unifies the entire Bible is the revealing of God's astounding plan for fixing everything we have messed up. The central figure in that plan is, of course, Immanuel, God with us, the great I AM, Jesus, God in human form. When Jesus walked among us, He said to those with a spiritual curiosity, "You search the Scriptures because you think that in them you have eternal life; *it is these that testify about Me*" (John 5:39, emphasis mine).

In the historical record of the gospel of Luke, he relates the events that occurred just after Jesus had risen from the dead. Jesus was walking on the road to a place called Emmaus with some of the disciples following along. They were oblivious to the fact that they were walking and talking with their risen Lord. Ponder that one awhile, thinking of your own life.

After it is clear that they were clueless about everything (remember, Jesus had told them in advance what was going to happen), Jesus says to them:

> "O foolish men and slow of heart to believe in all that the prophets have spoken! Was it not necessary for the Christ to suffer these things and to enter into His glory?" Then beginning with Moses and with all the prophets, He explained to them the things concerning Himself in all the Scriptures.
>
> Luke 24:25–27

First, consider how much of the New Testament would have been recorded at this point. Basically none. So Jesus uses the Old Testament to open the eyes of those who were blind to see the truth about who He really was. He wasn't simply a good teacher; a fine example; a docile, soft spoken itinerant; a prophet; a holy man. Jesus was God. He was there at creation, the Godhead, Three in One, bringing the universe into being.

> Then God said, "Let Us make man in Our image, according to Our likeness; and let them rule over the fish of the sea and over the birds of the sky and over the cattle and over all the earth, and over every creeping thing that creeps on the earth."
>
> Genesis 1:26

In Luke 16, Jesus tells the story about a man named Lazarus (this is not his good friend whom He resurrected from the grave) and a rich man. All we know is that this rich man is one who apparently obtained his best life now, being arrayed in the riches of the day. Jesus refers to Lazarus as "a certain beggar, full of sores and desiring to be fed with crumbs from the rich man's table" (Luke 16:20–21). (Poor Lazarus apparently failed to enlarge his vision.) Nevertheless, Jesus holds him up as the hero of the story.

So the two men are dead, and Jesus describes the difference in the two men's ultimate fate. The rich man was able to view the beggar man, Lazarus, being comforted by Abraham while he himself, after having his best life now, was tormented in Hades.

> And [*the rich man*] cried out and said, "Father Abraham, have mercy on me, and send Lazarus so that he may dip the tip of his finger in water and cool off my tongue, for I am in agony in this flame." But Abraham said, "Child, remember that during your life you received your good things, and likewise Lazarus bad things; but now he is being comforted here, and you are in agony."
>
> Luke 16:24–25

The rich man insisted on his rights, demanding Abraham give him some comfort as well, but the rich man's "seeing it, believing it, expecting it" fails to work in the afterlife. Abraham is unimpressed and says, "Child, remember that during your life you received your good things, and likewise Lazarus bad things; but now he is being comforted here, and you are in agony" (Luke 16:25).

I didn't cite this story to point out the irony of a mentality of acquiring one's best life now, and that certainly isn't why Jesus mentioned it. The punch line is coming.

The rich man, realizing he has been a fool in pursuing heaven on Earth, knows it is too late for him to change anything and, for the first time perhaps, experiences compassion for someone else, namely his family. He says, "Then I beg you, father, that you send him to my father's house—for I have five brothers—in order that he may warn them, so that they will not also come to this place of torment." But Abraham said, "They have Moses and the Prophets; let them hear them" (Luke 16:27–29).

What was the answer Abraham gave the rich man, more hoopla, more miracles, some magical water perhaps? Abraham says, "If they do not listen to Moses and the Prophets, they will not be persuaded even if someone rises from the dead" (Luke 16:31).

While many of today's Christians and "Christian" churches diminish, if not outright ignore, the Old Testament, Jesus didn't. The Old Testament was all about Jesus; the entire Bible is about Jesus first and foremost. Paul, writing to the Colossian believers, states, "[*Jesus*] is also head of the body, the church; and He is the beginning, the firstborn from the dead, so that He Himself will come to have first place in everything" (Colossians 1:18). Jesus! The preeminent One.

Listening to the prosperity preachers, reading their material, seeing how they work leads one to the inescapable conclusion that *God exists for me so that I can have it all now.* In the prosperity gospel, Jesus is not the preeminent One. My reason for existing is to talk myself and others into believing that everything promised to Adam and Eve prior to the fall at Eden is essentially available to me *now*. In the prosperity gospel, *I* am the preeminent one, and Jesus is my bondservant.

It is a dangerous practice isolating one fairly small element of the real gospel of Christ, pushing it to the center of everything as the be-all and end-all. But you cannot hear, see, or read the prosperity message and come away with anything other than self-absorption for the purpose of self-gratification.

The Self-Absorption of Prosperity

Pastor Osteen introduces the basic concept of the prosperity gospel, walking us through the evolution of when he and his wife acquired their dream home. It is at the center of everything. As a preacher, I am keenly aware of the value of using real-life illustrations to make my points clearer or more gripping. An axiom of good preaching is the more you can relate real-life application from your own experiences, the more approachable and credible your point is. That is their value. Using a real situation from one's own experience gives an authenticity to what otherwise might seem like nothing more than an unrealistic, even if nice, theory.

I do not fault the prosperity teachers for using real-life illustrations. To the contrary, I take them seriously, which is why the prosperity message so poignantly presented in *Your Best Life Now* is disturbing. Pastor Osteen writes:

Early in our marriage, Victoria and I were out walking through our neighborhood one day when we came upon a beautiful new home in the final stages of construction. The doors were open, so we stepped inside and looked around. It was fabulous home, much prettier than any of the other homes in that community. Most of the other homes around us were one-story, ranch style houses that were forty to fifty years old, but this house was a large two-story home, with high ceilings and over-sized windows providing an appealing view of the back yard. It was a lovely inspiring place.[46]

For the next several pages, the fulfillment of obtaining this house is the focus of their lives. He describes his lack of faith and his resistance to pursuing the obtainment of that house while his wife's great faith remained steadfast.

Victoria had much more faith than I did, and she would not give up…I told her all the reasons why I doubted. She said, "No Joel; I feel it deep inside. It is going to happen." She was so filled with joy, I didn't want to burst her bubble, so I let the matter drop. But Victoria didn't! Over the next several months, she kept speaking words of faith and victory, and she finally talked me into it. She convinced me that we could live in an elegant home like the one we saw. I got rid of my limited thinking and I started agreeing with her. I started believing that somehow, some way, God could bring it to pass. We kept on believing it, seeing it, and speaking it.[47]

The theme of acquiring their dream house, which they did ultimately obtain, is alluded to, returned to, and reiterated so often, conveying the message that the sum total of achievement, the key to happiness, the measure of success for the person of faith is in the goodies one procures here and now. In an ironic twist of orthodoxy, the bumper sticker I have seen that says, "The one who dies with the most toys wins," is apparently a good summation of the prosperity message. When I read the Bible, however, I find that the one who dies with the most toys *still* dies. Jesus seems to have thought similarly, as He told another parable in the twelfth chapter of Luke.

> The land of a rich man was very productive. And he began reasoning to himself, saying, "What shall I do, since I have no place to store my crops?" Then he said, "This is what I will do: I will tear down my barns and build larger ones, and there I will store all my grain and my goods. And I will say to my soul, 'Soul, you have many goods laid up for many years to come; take your ease, eat, drink and be merry.'" But God said to him, "You fool! This very night your soul is required of you; and now who will own what you have prepared?" So is the man who stores up treasure for himself, and is not rich toward God.
>
> Luke 12:16–21

In fairness, I must mention that the prosperity peddlers do, at times, talk of giving and benevolence. But even in this, they cannot seem to be able to avoid turning it to their advantage. That is, in order to *get* you have to *give*—and far more often than not, such giving is directed to the prosperity peddler's own ministry.

The pursuit of the perks this world has to offer is clearly the focus of the prosperites life, and that is the salient problem. Prosperity in and of itself is not inherently wrong. I do not share the mindset of the modern-day, guilt-heaping Christians who demand, "My conviction should be your conviction." I am hardly a modern-day ascetic, but there is a world—dare I say, an eternity—of difference in the proper pursuit of prosperity as a result of pursuing God as the center of your joy versus using God to pursue a prosperity that is the source of your joy. With the latter, the pursuit of prosperity becomes the defining feature of one's "new life in Christ." The "new life in Christ," though, is a life that is no longer dependant on the "things of this world" in order to be content and at peace.

C. S. Lewis states it clearly in his essay "Is Christianity Hard or Easy?"

> Christ says, "Give me ALL. I don't want just this much of your time and this much of your money and this much of your work—so that your natural self can have the rest. I want YOU. Not your things. I have come not to torture your natural self…I will give you a new self instead. Hand over the whole natural self—ALL the desires, not just the ones you think wicked but the ones you think innocent—the whole outfit."

The life blood of the prosperity gospel courses through the veins of self-interest, giving vitality and sustenance to the very self-centeredness that empowered our failure in the first place. But worse, the cross of the prosperity gospel is a cross of convenience, a cross of manipulation, and a cross devoid of sacrifice.

If Jesus had enlarged His vision instead of being obedient unto death, His kingdom would have been established, no doubt to the shouts of acclamation of the prosperites. But thank God He did not, for if Jesus had brought about His kingdom come, Gethsemane would have seen a night of solitude, the trials nonexistent, and the brutality unknown. If Jesus had brought about His kingdom come, the cross would have remained clean, the tomb unoccupied, and our experience of the eternal relegated to appropriated square footage, sparkling windows, and a nice yard.

The prosperity gospel is the very antithesis of the gospel of Christ. Instead of insisting the believer focuses on Jesus, it teaches we are to focus on who we want to be, what we want to have, and what we deserve as children of the King. Instead of considering ourselves and our desires *dead*, we are to energize, invigorate, and resuscitate the very base instincts that lead us away from God, the very base instincts from which Jesus came to set us free.

God's counsel is unmistakable, and it is diametrically opposed to the message of prosperity. Instead of enlarging our vision to name and claim the fulfillment of our very best here and now, we are to enlarge our vision as we grasp the magnitude of His vision for us.

Real prosperity then comes not in the acquisition of all *our* dreams as we expect it, believe it, see it, and speak it into existence. Real prosperity comes as we see who we have become *in Christ*. One demands we fix our gaze, our dreams, and our energies on all those things that are perishing and the other on the incomparable, awesome Savior and what His desires are for us to His glory and praise.

Paul explains to the Colossian believers:

> Therefore if you have been raised up with Christ, keep seeking the things above, where Christ is, seated at the right hand of God. Set your mind on the things above, not on the things that are on earth. For you have died and your life is hidden with Christ in God. When Christ, who is our life, is revealed, then you also will be revealed with Him in glory. Therefore consider the members of your earthly body as dead to immorality, impurity, passion, evil desire, and greed, which amounts to idolatry. For it is because of these things that the wrath of God will come upon the sons of disobedience, and in them you also once walked, when you were living in them.
>
> Colossians 3:1–7

"And in them you also once walked, when you were living in them." What God counsels us to bury in the past, the prosperity peddlers keep insisting we push into the present.

How have so many gotten so far off track? It is as simple as the siren call of self, playing the heartstrings of our innate (fallen) sense of who we are and who we trust. Jeremiah warned, "The heart is more deceitful than all else and is desperately corrupt; who can understand it?" (Jeremiah 17:9). Obviously not us. Every step along the way of life, I am prone to go with "what my heart tells me." It is the prevailing attitude of our day, both inside and outside the church.

Yet Jeremiah continues: "I, the Lord, search the heart, I test the mind, even to give to each man according to his ways, according to the results of his deeds (Jeremiah 17:10).

God is the only one we can and should trust. We simply are too easily led astray.

Robert Robinson penned the words acknowledging our inclination toward self-centered autonomy. The hymn "Come Thou Fount of Every Blessing" shows that in 1758, before technology, before the Internet and e-mail, prior to Facebook and Twitter, the human spirit has always been in a pugilistic struggle for control of our loyalties and our decision-making authority.

> O to grace how great a debtor
>
> Daily I'm constrained to be!
>
> Let Thy goodness, like a fetter,
>
> Bind my wandering heart to Thee.
>
> Prone to wander, Lord, I feel it,
>
> Prone to leave the God I love;
>
> Here's my heart, O take and seal it,
>
> Seal it for Thy courts above.

The solution is not found in the snake oil of the prosperity gospel but in the gospel of Jesus itself. It is to abandon our heart's desires, surrendering our thoughts, our passions, our aspirations, and our dreams unto the One who purchased our souls for Himself. We have, after all, "been bought with a price"—the price of Jesus's own blood (1 Corinthians 6:20). In one of the many ironies of God's truth, Jesus informs us that to find one's self, one must lose himself. This goes against everything we are, naturally speaking, which is why even a whisper of affirmation to the desires of self will be heard above the shouts of truth from God's spirit. Unfortunately, the prosperity gospel is what we *want* to hear.

When the serpent hissed his challenge to Eve, it was not an all-out frontal assault on her intelligence and ability to reason. He simply catered to her wants, inserting doubt in her mind about what she had been told by God. "Indeed, has God said, 'You shall not eat from any tree of the garden'?" (Genesis 3:1). With what seemed to be reasonable doubt presented to Eve, implying she must have misunderstood what God really said, the fruit wasn't the only thing ripe for the picking. "When the woman saw that the tree was good for food, and that it was a delight to the eyes, and that the tree was desirable to make one wise, she took from its fruit and ate..." (Genesis 3:6)

What's the formula for delusion? Take the Word of God, manipulate it slightly this way or that, and then speak affirming language that plays right into what one wants to hear. It is not a new strategy. But in the case of the peddlers of prosperity, it is effective, even though it is blatantly opposed to the wondrous liberating perspective spoken by Jesus Himself.

> For this reason I say to you, do not worry about your life, as to what you will eat; nor for your body, as to what you will put on. For life is more than food, and the body more than clothing. Consider the ravens, for they neither sow nor reap; they have no storeroom, nor barn, and yet God feeds them; how much more valuable you are than the birds! And which of you by worrying can add a single hour to his life's span? If then you cannot do even a very little thing, why do you worry about other matters? Consider the lilies, how they grow: they neither toil nor spin; but I tell you, not even

Solomon in all his glory clothed himself like one of these. But if God so clothes the grass in the field, which is alive today and tomorrow is thrown into the furnace, how much more will He clothe you? You men of little faith! And do not seek what you will eat and what you will drink, and do not keep worrying. For all these things the nations of the world eagerly seek; but your Father knows that you need these things. But seek His kingdom, and these things will be added to you.

Luke 12:16–31

17

THE PROPER PERSPECTIVE ON PROSPERITY

In previous chapters, I have referred to the partial truth, the kernel of truth, and the balanced truth. In the interest of balanced biblical accuracy, it is important to understand that there *is* a real present-day experience, even expectation, of prosperity. Nevertheless, it is vastly different than the prosperity proclaimed by the prosperity preachers today. It will be helpful at this point if you suspend your preconceived Western notions of prosperity or it will seem I am contradicting what I have already written.

When someone orders their life under the Lordship of Jesus, "prosperity" is a by-product. That is, the blessing (prosperity) of God truly follows obedience. But this kind of prosperity is not the fulfillment of wishful thinking. It is not an utterly self-absorbed passion for self-gratification and for everything this world has to offer. Rather, this prosperity is much more akin to the Jewish concept of *shalom*.

Even Gentiles today might utter the word as a token of kind consideration or blessing toward someone. At a base level, *shalom* means "peace." But this peace is much deeper than merely the absence of turmoil or strife in one's life. The broad meaning of *shalom* connotes the oversight, guidance, and generous blessing of God on every part of a person's existence. It *might* include financial increase; after all, some of the faithful followers of God in the Bible were well-off or even obscenely rich. Who today, regardless of their religious stripe, does not associate Solomon with fortunes similar to Bill Gates or Warren Buffet? Indeed, many of the patriarchs in the Old Testament were wealthy. And while there is geo-socio-cultural adaptation as the Christian Church begins to multiply and spread, the Scriptures do not ever excoriate the quality of personal affluence per se. Neither do the Scriptures ever quantify what constitutes a godly net worth. Contrary to popular belief, the Bible does not say, "Money is the root of all evil," but rather, "The *love* of money is the root of all evil" (1 Timothy 6:10).

It is not having possessions that are wrong but the passionate pursuit of possessions as a goal, as a focus of one's life that is terribly misguided. It is not having possessions that are wrong, but it is being possessed by those possessions and their pursuit as a lifestyle goal that is lethal.

The well-known story of the one who is popularly called the rich young ruler illustrates the point poignantly.

> A ruler questioned Him, saying, "Good Teacher, what shall I do to inherit eternal life?" And Jesus said to him, "Why do you call Me good? No one is

good except God alone. You know the command-
ments, 'Do not commit adultery, do not murder,
do not steal, do not bear false witness, honor your
father and mother.'" And he said, "All these things
I have kept from my youth." When Jesus heard
this, He said to him, "One thing you still lack; sell
all that you possess and distribute it to the poor,
and you shall have treasure in heaven; and come,
follow Me." But when he had heard these things,
he became very sad, for he was extremely rich. And
Jesus looked at him and said, "How hard it is for
those who are wealthy to enter the kingdom of
God! For it is easier for a camel to go through the
eye of a needle than for a rich man to enter the
kingdom of God."

Luke 18:18–25

The story is not about one's net worth as if being rich is
inherently sinful. The story is not an indictment against
those with comfortable incomes or even lavish surroundings. It is about maintaining the proper priorities of life,
the prosper pursuit of prosperity. After all, the history of
the human race provides ample evidence that affluence
tends to chisel away at one's closeness to God. Apostasy
(falling away from God) is not a necessary outcome, but
as mentioned earlier, it is certainly an often repeated
outcome evidenced through the ages. God's people
throughout the Old Testament tended to fare well when
they were in fairly dire straits. When the pressure was
off, and when the circumstances of life were more favor-
able, there was a lessened need for the Almighty.

The wild success of Solomon, who clearly had his
best life now, was precisely what brought about his undo-
ing. Philip Yancey writes in *Disappointment with God*:

> In one generation Solomon took Israel from a
> fledgling kingdom dependent on God for bare sur-
> vival to a self-sufficient political power. But along
> the way he lost sight of the original vision to which
> God had called them...Success in the kingdom of
> this world had crowded out interest in the king-
> dom of God.[48]

As you follow God's people through the wilderness, relative prosperity tends to precede spiritual decline. It is
easy to trust in a God when you are at the end of your
resources and abilities. You really have little choice. It
is altogether another adventure to trust in God when
you have everything you need and, even worse, when
you have everything you can envision. Yancey notes
this speaking of Solomon's collapse. "Success may have
eliminated any crises of [*Solomon's*] disappointment with
God, but it also seemed to eliminate Solomon's desire for
God at all. The more he enjoyed the world's good gifts,
the less he thought about the Giver."[49]

As I took my noon break to exercise, I was again
channel surfing, scanning yet more prosperity prosely-
tizers, when I stumbled on the first peddler—one with
whom I was unfamiliar—telling the viewers he was
going to send you "these gifts," holding what looked like
a stack of booklets, pamphlets, and CDs. Then he continued that these "gifts" would be yours when you send
in $40. *Click.* I moved on.

The next preacher I landed on—another unfamiliar name in the pantheon of prosperity peddlers—was
hawking his five-day "Best Life Now" cruise. No, it
wasn't Joel Osteen. (Apparently when you "enlarge your

vision," furthering your own prosperity by riding the coattails of someone else's is fair game.)

From what I have seen, read, and heard, the purveyors of prosperity enjoin their followers to pursue God *not* because of Who He is but for what He can give them. The pursuit of God's kingdom and righteousness is for little more than obtaining the competitive edge one acquires when he learns how to manipulate God for one's own purposes and joy. Timothy Keller in *The Reason for God* sees it differently:

> If we will center our lives on him, serving him not out of self-interest, but just for the sake of who he is, for the sake of his beauty and glory, we will dance and share in the joy and love he lives in. We were designed, then, not just for belief in God in some general way nor for a vague kind of inspiration or spirituality. We were made to center our lives upon him, to make the purpose and passion of our lives knowing, serving, delighting, and resembling him.[50]

Recently, I was reflecting on the warning issued by James in his eponymous book where he writes, "Let not many of you become teachers, my brethren, knowing that as such we will incur a stricter judgment" (James 3:1).

As a man who has been teaching in the church for over two decades and who has been teaching through the print media for nearly as long, it is sobering to consider that such a warning was not placed there to fill space. I have to wonder if the "professors" of prosperity are ever inclined to inquisitively wonder beyond their own apparent "success" contemplating their ultimate accountability.

What are we to make of our lot in life? Do we glibly accept our station in life almost like the caste system of Hinduism? Is it wrong to be aggressive, to be diligent, to work hard, and to be focused with lofty goals and high aspirations? Not only is it not wrong, but it is appropriate as long as one keeps the perspective that every element of the believer's life is subject to review and approval by the one called LORD.

Many in the church today are satisfied living with the God of heaven and earth as their personal Savior, but personal LORD is another issue. Sadly, the sentiment reflected in the bumper sticker, "God is my co-pilot," is all too true.

18

GOD WANTS TO PROSPER US PROPERLY

Delight yourself in the LORD; And He will give
you the desires of your heart. Commit your way
to the LORD, Trust also in Him, and He will do it.

Psalm 37:4–5

I mentioned earlier my aspirations for medical school.
With a bit of desperation, I made a prayer deal with
God—something I do not recommend—saying that I
would make application to only one medical school and
only one time. I would accept the outcome as God's
direction for my life. What I never anticipated was the
head of the admissions committee taking me aside, saying, "While I can't guarantee anything, if for some reason you don't get in this year, reapply next year, and I
don't think you will be disappointed."

Anyone else would have been elated, an essential
promise of their dream being laid out for them on a sil-
ver platter. I, on the other hand, was sick to my stom-

ach. Remember, my prayer to God was one time, one school—that would be the end of it.

I set out for my intended goal but each step had to undergo the scrutiny of my God, who is both Lord and Savior. My ideas of prosperity for me and my family are only as clear as my limited foresight allows as a very flawed human being. I pledged allegiance to the Lord the day I said, "I do," to His Lordship in my life. As my life was developing, often unknown to me, God was shaping and molding me for other purposes than relieving physical ailments of others. When the time came to make the final decision on my road to medicine, the Lordship of the One who purchased my life at a great price made it clear that He had different plans for me—plans to give me a future and a hope as defined by the One whose love and best for me are unquestionable. God delights to prosper us according to His intimate knowledge of those who love Him, even as David reveals in the Psalm 37.

Psalm 37:4 is the kind of verse that inspires passion in the proponents of the prosperity gospel: "God will give you the desires of your heart!" As it is abused by the peddlers of an improper prosperity, this snippet does contain the kernel of truth, but the passage has to be taken on balance. There are major qualifications contained in the text concerning God fulfilling His part of the promise.

The first one mentioned is delighting yourself in the Lord. If one is captivated by, thrilled by, indeed in love with the Lord, the desires of that one's heart will reflect the desires not of their own heart but of God's own heart. That in and of itself eliminates any preponderance of frivolous or self-centered wishes.

The next qualification says, "Commit your way to the LORD, Trust also in Him, and He will do it" (Psalm 37:5). Dreams are fine, even wishes are fun, as long as both are always subject unto the final wisdom of God, who knows us better than we know ourselves. He made us. If anyone knows what will truly bless us, will truly bring us joy, accomplishment, and peace, it is the One who created us. So my desires for medical school were admirable, and I committed those plans to Him. I know He loves me and wants only my very best. At the end of the day, it was easy to trust my legacy, my future, and my family's future to the One who knows me best and has my best interests at heart. If those conditions are met, God, to be sure, will give us the desires of our heart.

True prosperity—a prosperity that is proper—comes in submitting to the Lordship of a loving Savior, not making demands for things that will perish.

The course of my life had to be changed because in Christ, my life is not *my* life. Was I disappointed? Candidly, yes. But surpassing my disappointment was my confidence and peace that God knows what He's doing and because He loves me, I could trust Him. That makes all the difference.

During this particular time in my life, I had no aspiration or a single thought concerning the ministry. I couldn't possibly have anticipated the surpassing joy of investing my life in seeing people healed for eternity rather than just for a momentary season on this side of heaven. Does this mean I never have second thoughts? Not at all.

There is a scene in the movie version of *Chariots of Fire* where Olympian runner Eric Liddell discovers, after the fact, that one of his qualifying heats is to be run on a Sunday. Liddell, being a man of tremendous faith and conviction, informs the Olympic committee that he cannot run due to his beliefs about honoring the Sabbath. As he is sitting in the stands on that Sunday, watching the race he should have been running in, a friend leans over and asks, "Any regrets?" Liddell responds, "Yeah, but no doubts!"

As I was growing up and going through different phases of "What will I be when I grow up?" my mother used to say to me, "I don't care if you're a garbage collector, but you need to be the best garbage collector there is!" Wanting to be the best one can be and desiring to rise in one's field of endeavor is actually a precept of biblical wisdom. Paul is writing to believers in Colossae, addressing husbands, wives, children, fathers, and even slaves, telling them what their attitude should be, no matter where their position in life happens to land.

"Whatever you do, do your work heartily, as for the Lord rather than for men, knowing that from the Lord you will receive the reward of the inheritance. It is the Lord Christ whom you serve" (Colossians 3:23–24).

Do you see the difference in the message of the inspired Word of God as opposed to the message of the prosperity scammers? In the Word, being the best, working hard, trying to get ahead, and improving your station is motivated by the very idea that it is actually God for Whom you are working. Trying to shine is for the very purpose of reflecting the brilliance of God. It is knowing that what you do and how you do it is important to God and that what you do truly is a reflection on Him and hopefully of Him.

When I was going through seminary in suburban Chicago, my wife took a part-time job as a waitress. She would come home and tell me her war stories of interesting people she waited on, as well as the unruly children who left tornado-like devastation in their wake. They were extra work, but that was the job. More trying than the bouncing barbarians were the cranky Christians. She said the general rule among the wait staff at the restaurant was that no one wanted to work Sundays because that was the church crowd. Her colleagues informed her, "They are loud, impatient, demanding, and they are poor tippers."

As a pastor, I have always been sensitive to stereotypes of those in my position. Becoming a pastor later in life, I had enough experience as a churchgoer to have a pretty good feel for why Christians in general and pastors in particular can have less-than-admirable reputations.

Shortly after moving to the town where I have been ministering for two decades, a man shared with me that he had been hired to install a new furnace system for the pastor of his church. (Installing heating systems is what the man did to put food on the table and pay his bills.) When it came time to settle up, the pastor told this man that he should not be charging him since he was his pastor. That is unconscionable.

Before ever going into ministry, I had also heard that pastors are notorious for being slow to pick up a check at a restaurant and even expecting that when they go out to lunch with someone, the someone will pick up the check. So I made it my personal policy that whenever I went to eat with someone—including other pastors—whether I initiated the appointment or not, I would pick up the check (and leave a generous tip). There have been several times I noticed that people were surprised by this, and sometimes I had to do considerable persuading that I really wanted to pay for the meal. To me, it was a matter of personal integrity, but more, it was a matter of honoring the Lord. Honestly, I enjoyed being able to pick up the tab for some pretty well-off men back in the days when the church couldn't even afford to pay me a livable wage. But it apparently was a blessing to the Lord, as He made sure we never suffered financially on account of it. In fact, He prospered us in faithfulness, in joy, and even financially. So I readily acknowledge and celebrate there is a certain dimension of prosperity—even material prosperity—that is part and parcel of the gospel, but prosperity is not *the* gospel.

It would also be foolish to deny that there is no connection between faithful obedience and God's physical/ material blessing. You cannot read the Old Testament for very long without seeing a clear pattern God establishes of, "If you do this, I will do that."

> It shall come about, if you listen obediently to my commandments which I am commanding you today, to love the LORD your God and to serve Him with all your heart and all your soul, that He will give the rain for your land in its season, the early and late rain, that you may gather in your grain and your new wine and your oil. He will give grass in your fields for your cattle, and you will eat and be satisfied.
>
> Deuteronomy 11:13–15

The same basic formula is reestablished in the gospels. After Jesus admonishes His followers about the proper perspective on the necessities of life, He concludes with the all-important apex of the pattern.

> Do not worry then, saying, "What will we eat?" or "What will we drink?" or "What will we wear for clothing?" For the Gentiles eagerly seek all these things; for your heavenly Father knows that you need all these things. But seek first His kingdom and His righteousness, and all these things will be added to you.
>
> Matthew 6:31–33

"Seek *first* His Kingdom…" In other words, make God's priorities your priorities, and similarly, "Seek *first* His righteousness…" That is, endeavor to allow God to shape Himself within you, to make His heart your heart, to make His burdens your burdens, and to make His dreams your dreams. When Jesus taught us to pray, he instructed, "*Thy* kingdom come, *Thy* will be done…" The prosperity gospel, with its promises of an improper prosperity, turns this all upside down, insisting *my* priorities are God's priorities, *my* dreams are His dreams, and that when I pray the prayer of faith, it is essentially *my* kingdom come, *my* will be done.

Is God faithful to bless the proper pursuit of prosperity, or what I would call the Christian's pure efforts to pursue God's priorities? Absolutely, and even beyond what our puny little minds think might be great. But that doesn't mean every whim we have, every want we express, every physical or material goodie we can imagine is ours by right.

As a loving parent of three and now a grandparent of nine, even I know that not everything my children and grandchildren want would make them happy, even though they think it might. What child, if given the choice, would refuse the chocolate-covered doughnut with sprinkles for the bowl of gray, murky oatmeal? And if given that kind of choice whenever one of my grandsons or granddaughters wanted it, they would habitually choose what I know to be a poor choice. So as a loving grandparent, I refrain from indulging them—sometimes even though it pains me—because I know in the long run, they will be better off not getting everything they demand. By the same token, I am going to bend over backward to give my children and grandchildren what they desire if it is good for them. We are told God is the same way with us.

> Or what man is there among you who, when his son asks for a loaf, will give him a stone? Or if he asks for a fish, he will not give him a snake, will he? If you then, being evil, know how to give good gifts to your children, how much more will your Father who is in heaven give what is good to those who ask Him!
>
> Matthew 7:9–11

Because God loves us, He delights in giving us good things, but God is never obligated to fulfill our wishes, dreams, and demands, no matter how much faith we claim, no matter how many times we speak the desire believing it fulfilled. That is not faith; that is witchcraft. When Paul writes the Philippian believers, he says, "Have no anxieties about anything, but in everything by prayer and supplication with thanksgiving let your requests be made known to God" (Philippians 4:6).

If I were one of the peddlers of prosperity, I would leave the verse on its own two feet and drive it into the ground, insisting that God has given us His credit card to the universe which has no limit. And then—in the words of Pastor Osteen—I just need to "believe it, see it, and speak it" and it will come about. But the letter to the believers at Philippi continues: "And the peace of God, which surpasses all understanding, will keep your hearts and your minds in Christ Jesus" (Philippians 4:7).

Notice there is no guarantee that by bringing all your requests (not demands) to the Lord, they will be fulfilled as you think they should be fulfilled. What is guaranteed is that when you bring everything that burdens you to the loving, all-knowing, all-powerful God, you will be released from the troubling, consuming nature of whatever seems to be so important to you. God will grant His peace (*shalom*)—no matter what the situation—and He will strap you to His side, so to speak, so that you won't wander off when things don't go your way. Neither will you slide into depression when you do not get what you want. That is, He will give you His perspective in the matter, and in that, there will be contentment, if not release, from all that might otherwise rob you of abundance in life.

Now compare the arrogantly assuming hearts and minds of the prosperity prophets to the faith-filled, prayerful hearts of Shadrach, Meshach, and Abed-nego, who we find in a tight spot in the book of Daniel.

They had just refused to bow in worship to King Nebuchadnezzar's gods. The penalty for refusal to do so was execution by burning. The king asks if they are ready to comply and worship his idol. Their response is laudable:

> Shadrach, Meshach and Abed-nego replied to the king, "O Nebuchadnezzar, we do not need to give you an answer concerning this matter. If it be so, our God whom we serve is able to deliver us from the furnace of blazing fire; and He will deliver us out of your hand, O king…"

It would be characteristic of the prosperity preachers to stop there and use this as proof of the power of proclamation. But to do so would be presumptuous to say the least. The verse continues, "But even if He does not, let it be known to you, O king, that we are not going to serve your gods or worship the golden image that you have set up" (Daniel 3:16–18).

In a modern context, the priests and priestesses of prosperity I have been listening to would likely declare such a statement a betrayal of faith. In reality, Shadrach, Meshach, and Abed-nego simply knew their place in the grand scheme of things and were ready to trust their fate to the hands of the One who created them. Come what may, they served a powerful God of love and nothing changed that, not even if forfeiting their lives turned out to be the reward for their faithfulness.

Shadrach, Meshach, and Abed-nego were walking in the proper pursuit of prosperity. In the *shalom* of God, they had a peace and a contentment as they lived and breathed and had their being under the watchful eye of a God who knew them and who loved them. That love and peace did not need lavish surroundings or even the promise of the preservation of life. The true prosperity that is part and parcel of the gospel of Christ *might* include physical preservation and material increase, but real gospel prosperity is well beyond such narrow trivialities as an increase in pay, a new title, or a second home. The psalmist must have been living in the prosperity of *shalom* when he penned the following:

> For a day in Your courts is better than a thousand outside. I would rather be a doorkeeper in the house of my God than dwell in the tents of wickedness. For the LORD God is a sun and shield; The LORD gives grace and glory; No good thing does He withhold from those who walk uprightly. O LORD of hosts, how blessed [*how Shalom-ed*] is the man who trusts in You!
>
> Psalm 84:10–12

The *shalom* greeting of the Jewish faithful is a wish for God's best in all ways. The proper pursuit of prosperity then brings us into that *shalom*, and we begin living life as God would want us to live it with a constant view to living it for Him.

19

SOMETIMES PROSPERITY HIDES UNDER ADVERSITY

Sometimes the blessing of prosperity is not readily apparent. These are the times that challenge one's faith. These are the times Satan loves to invade our thoughts planting seeds of doubt, asking, "Did God really say ...?" In these times, what it comes down to is who or what will be the authoritative or influential foundation of my existence—that is, who or what will define my view of my circumstances and my well-being. For Job's wife, it was the authority or influence of the crisis. Her encouragement to her husband was, "Curse God and die" (Job 2:9). Had Job listened to his wife, if he had tuned in to the cacophony of the calamity, he would have succumbed to Satan's plan; Satan would have won.

Job's challenge was the same one we face every time the circumstances of the moment conflict with our desire, namely, "Am I going to trust in the voice and nature of my circumstances, or am I going to trust in the voice and the nature of my God?" It is a choice that everyone

makes every day of their lives. Stated more simply, "Do I
trust my circumstances and react to them in human wisdom, or do I trust my God and react in godly wisdom?"
Job chose wisely, but for most of us, the inconvenience of
hardship strangles the prosperity of God's *shalom*, which,
in turn, hampers our ability to listen. Still, sometimes
God's presence is so compelling that it requires effort
not to listen.

Not long after I had been working as a medical technologist, I received a phone call totally out of the blue
from an old friend from my days in the army. We kept in
touch at Christmastime, but that was about it. He was
working as a chaplain in a Washington state hospital and
called to ask me if I had any interest in hospital administration. I think I said I wasn't even sure what it was
but not really. We were happy where we were in Atlanta,
although I was looking to the future as far as my career
in medical technology. Being a predominantly female-
oriented allied health career, the pay was not great (this
was the late '70s), so I had my sights set on the headquarters of the Center for Disease Control (CDC) in
Atlanta. As a government service employee, there was
much better potential for advancement.

At any rate, my friend said that his boss, the administrator of Auburn General Hospital, might give me
a call to chat about a career change. It was a strange
call, but I relayed to my wife what was going on. Even
though we had no desire to make a career change, much
less pack up and move our young family of four (with
a third child on the way) across the country, we both
knew in our spirits we would be moving to Seattle. We
never shared this with each other until much later. After

a couple phone calls from the hospital's head administrator, Barbara and I were on our way to a job interview in the Pacific Northwest.

Bill Erickson was a soft-spoken, gentlemanly Christian in his mid to late '60s. After explaining to this man my utter lack of education, desire, and experience in hospital administration, he said, "Let's go back to my hotel room and spend some time in prayer." Thus began another adventure into the unknown yet knowing we were being directed by the hand of God.

Literally over night, I moved from a white lab coat shaking test tubes to sitting in my own office, wearing a three-piece suit, staring at the wall, asking out loud to the air, "What am I doing here, God?" Yet after nine months as the administrative assistant to the hospital administrator, I was promoted to assistant administrator of ancillary services. I was assigned responsibility for six departments and was being groomed for the future replacement of the administrator, who was set to retire in just a couple years. But there was a fly in the ointment.

Unknown to me, the hospital (previously a not-for-profit organization) had been in secret negotiations to be sold to a proprietary health care corporation. Within a matter of months, I had a new, inexperienced thirty-two-year-old boss out to make a name for himself at any cost. Unlike the Christian hospital organization I had signed on with, this organization had one purpose for existing: maximizing profit, no matter who or what was trampled in the process.

It was readily apparent I would not be able to continue working for my new employers while maintaining a clear conscience. I began considering my next step in life. The same friend who started this whole adventure by calling me that day in Atlanta asked, "If you could do anything you wanted, what would you do?" By this time, my wife and I had been followers of Jesus ten years, and it was obvious that we were being used by the Lord to gather people around us, studying the Bible with them and coaching them in life's issues—in short, making other followers of Jesus. I answered, "I would like to go to seminary to become a pastor." In reality, that was just a pipe dream. Like so many in life, we were trapped by obligation. I couldn't just walk away from a good-paying job until I had something else on which to rely. We had a mortgage with a 15½ percent interest rate, and the housing market in Seattle was bust with another downturn of the Boeing Corporation, one of the area's major employers.

As I entered work one morning, I was informed that the hospital had failed several portions of the inspection by the Joint Commission for the Accreditation of Hospitals (JCAH). Failing the re-inspection of a JCAH inspection was not an option. A hospital's financial viability rests on it for failing to pass has reimbursement ramifications with Medicare and others. Though none of my departments were on the casualty list, my new boss brought me into his office and told me he wanted me to take all the delinquent medical records that caused us to fail that portion of the inspection and make them disappear. I saw my career flash before my eyes. Doing what he asked would be a felony.

In that instant, I remembered Joseph and his temptation with Potiphar's wife (Genesis 39). Pastor and author Gordon McDonald, in a message I heard him give over a decade earlier entitled "Cutting out Lions," asked, "If Joseph had caved in that day to Potiphar's wife, would he have been the kind of man God could have used to become prime minister and literally the savior of the nations?" (a close paraphrase) More than anything, I wanted to be God's man on whom He could rely, no matter what.

Sitting in front of my boss, I paused for a moment and said respectfully, "Mark, you know I can't do that." He vigorously shook his head, saying, "Oh, I understand. Okay…" That was at about 11:30 in the morning. When I came back from lunch, there was an envelope waiting on my desk with a letter charging me with everything that had ever been wrong with the hospital long before I even worked there and a severance check. I was stunned to be sure, and yet I was not shaken. In fact, I was honestly relieved. I went home and told my wife that we were no longer encumbered by a job. Being obedient in this life does not guarantee justice in this world turned upside down by sin.

We made plans to sell our home, returning to the Midwest to a seminary I heard had a great reputation for being a rigorously biblical institution where they taught people how to think, not just what to think. Even though the admissions deadline was past for the coming school year in September, I was notified that I was accepted. Now all we needed was to sell our new home in a matter of a few weeks, on a loan assumption, at 15½ percent interest, in order to make enough money to move back to Chicago to begin another new adventure at Trinity Evangelical Divinity School. How we would sell our home in such a depressed economy; where we would live once we arrived in Chicago; and how we would pay for what we later learned was one of the most expensive seminaries in the country? These were problems for the Mastermind of our future. We knew what the Lord wanted, and that was all that mattered.

> "For I know the plans that I have for you," declares the LORD, "plans for welfare and not for calamity to give you a future and a hope."
>
> Jeremiah 29:11

The authority of God surpassed the authority of my circumstances, and God's prosperity—*God's shalom*—reigned supreme.

On the last day that I determined we would need to know who our home buyer would be in order to make all the deadlines for school, a man drove by in his Jeep, saw our "for sale by owner" sign, stopped, looked around, and faster than you can say, "We're moving," assumed our outrageous loan and bought our house for what we were asking without even trying to offer less.

Contrary to the tenets of current prosperity protocol, I can honestly say it was not because of my faith but in spite of my lack of faith that our house sold as we desired.

God knows what He's about, and our faith, or lack thereof, will not hinder the Master of the universe. If I got what I expected, as one of the prosperity gospel axioms teach, we would still be in Seattle, probably panhandling on the street.

Under God's watchful eye, we packed, moved, found a rental house in a comfortable northwest suburb of Chicago, and I matriculated at Trinity like clockwork.

God blesses what God is about, and obstacles for us are no obstacles for Him.

Each time God interposes in the affairs of our lives, we would do well to recount His faithful intrusions. The more we stay mindful of His faithfulness—often in spite of our faithlessness—the stronger we are when facing the next hurdle.

In the days of Samuel the priest, God's people were facing insurmountable odds against the Philistines at Mizpah. Samuel offered sacrifices to God, asking for His favor and help. God graciously answered, routing their enemies in sound defeat. Instead of giving rousing rounds of congratulatory accolades to each other for their battlefield prowess, Samuel made certain they did not quickly forget exactly Who the reason was for their success. He took a stone and set it up as a memorial. In the language of the day, "Eben-ezer" is actually two words, which mean "stone of help." The stone of help takes on the meaning of a rock of remembrance, acting much like a statue or monument that is erected today to cause people to remember something or someone important.

> Then Samuel took a stone and set it between Mizpah and Shen, and named it Ebenezer, saying, "Thus far the LORD has helped us." So the Philistines were subdued and they did not come anymore within the border of Israel. And the hand of the LORD was against the Philistines all the days of Samuel.
>
> 1 Samuel 7:12–13

In 1758, Robert Robinson penned the words to a hymn familiar to older generations titled, "Come Thou Fount of Every Blessing." The second verse contains the allusion to 1 Samuel 7, noting that it is solely by God's good graces that any of us gain eternity.

> Sorrowing I shall be in spirit,
>
> 'Till released from flesh and sin,
>
> Yet from what I do inherit,
>
> Here Thy praises I'll begin;
>
> Here I raise my Ebenezer;
>
> Here by Thy great help I've come;
>
> And I hope, by Thy good pleasure,
>
> Safely to arrive at home.

Looking back and recounting the places in your life where you have recognized that God has been gracious and good is an effective way of raising an Ebenezer. With such remembrances comes strength to face the daunting circumstances of living in a fallen world. It is an effective way of appropriating God's proper prosperity instead of making foolish demands born out of foolish egos.

God's Prosperity Is Truly Miraculous

Barbara and my heart's desire, believing it is consistent with God's plan for families, is that children are supposed to be raised by their parents, not hired laborers. With our Ebenezers raised, we trusted that in some way, God would allow me to go to school full time, coming home in the afternoon to stay with our children while my wife went to waitress part time in the evenings. Her income certainly would not keep our ship afloat, but I also had about a year left on the remainder of my GI bill. It paid us several hundred dollars a month. As I wrote earlier, we were always committed to honoring the Lord with a tithe of our income, and we did so throughout seminary, joyfully giving 10 percent of our meager and inadequate income to the Lord. During this time, my dentist from Seattle, who was a fellow follower of Jesus, faithfully sent us $100 each month. It was a miracle how far God stretched those dollars. When I needed extra income for books, a check would show up in the mail from someone in our past that "felt moved to send us something."

When our meager savings from the sale of our house was expended, we were just a couple weeks away from another tuition payment—a payment we did not have. Barb was waitressing that weekend, and her folks came in to have breakfast. They dropped a tip of $2,000. We didn't solicit these funds. That was not our way. We did not visualize the amount we needed nor insist, in faith, that God meet our demand. God just knew our need, and this was His program. He makes it work. To this day, I cannot explain it, but when I finished Trinity two years later (I attended year round and took overload schedules) we were debt-free.

> Bring the whole tithe into the storehouse, so that there may be food in My house, and test Me now in this, says the LORD of hosts, if I will not open for you the windows of heaven and pour out for you a blessing until it overflows.
>
> Malachi 3:10

I call it God's math. There *is* prosperity in aligning one's life call and purpose with the call and purpose of God for you. This is what it means to "seek first the kingdom of God..." (Matthew 6:33). It is not because I can demand it being a child of the King; it is not because I "see it, believe it, and expect it." It is because central to the gospel of redemption is that God is our friend and God loves His friends. He lavishes His good graces in this life on whomever He will for His purposes, not ours.

There were still plenty of challenges facing us as we patiently waited for our next epoch in life. I was finished with seminary and was waiting for the right church situation to come along. I was not looking for a job; I was waiting for God's matchmaking, fitting us where He would put us next. I never anticipated that the "temporary" job I took after seminary in a plastics factory in suburban Chicago would drag on for several years. I graduated from Trinity in the winter of '85, but it wasn't until after a stint as a bi-vocational pastor, as well as starting a church out of our home in Chicago, that my first "real" church called five years later.

The day we received the first phone call of inquiry about the church in Maine, my wife and I, independent of each other, knew we would be moving to New England. It was truly a match made in heaven. It was not only love at first sight, but I am writing this book while on sabbatical celebrating my twentieth year with my greatly enlarged family at Faith Evangelical Free Church. The church that started as thirty-seven men, women, and children when my wife and children arrived has long since outgrown our little converted duplex of a church building to a retrofitted Cineplex we now own. But those early days were wonderful, even though challenging.

Upon arriving in Maine, we moved into the basement of dear people from the church until we could find a place of our own. Down the street was a century-old New England farmhouse on which the bank had foreclosed. I went to talk to the bank about buying it, never having seen the house on the inside since people were still living there illegally.

The bank was eager to divest themselves of the property, but there was one small problem. The income our small church was able to pay our family of five was hardly livable, much less adequate to buy a house, even a foreclosure. But our experience with the God of the impossible gave us confidence that He had it figured out, especially when we didn't.

I sat across the desk from the banker examining our numbers. He said there was no way he could work something out. I remembered not speaking much. I was busy shooting into the air what the great Dallas professor Howard Hendricks calls "sky telegrams." I remember silently praying, "Lord, you know we need a place to live ..."

The banker kept clicking away on his calculator and each time would pause, staring at his figures and shaking his head, negatively saying, "I just don't see how we can do anything." I remained quietly praying. After about the fifth attempt on his calculator, he looked up and said, "Here's what I am going to do. I am going to give you an in-house loan." I wasn't even sure what that meant, but it sounded good. With that, on a handshake, he said, "Get your family moved in and we'll worry about paperwork later when you get settled."

A couple days later, we moved our furnishings into this house. The downstairs was in good shape, though strangely configured. The upstairs, on the other hand, was down to the studs, wires hanging out of the walls. One of the stairways (there were two in this lovely old home) was absent with just a shaft from the basement to the second floor. The opening to this shaft on the second floor had a piece of sheetrock leaning against it to keep the toddler who lived there from falling into the abyss. One of the bedrooms on the second floor had an old-fashioned hexagonal coffin in it and was painted black with "Dr. Death" stenciled in red to look like blood was dripping from the words. (Apparently, one of the teens who lived in the house was in a heavy metal band, and this was a stage prop. That was a relief.)

None of this mattered to us. We were in the home God provided, and we were thrilled. Later that day, the man from the bank stopped by to see how we were doing, and when he walked in, his chin hit the floor. He was utterly dismayed, saying he had no idea the house was in the kind of shape it was. He kept apologizing and then said, "I am going to give you another twenty thousand dollars because you are going to have to put some money into this place."

Within just a couple weeks' time, our house was transformed, and when we eventually ended up signing a conventional loan some years later, our thirty-year mortgage was paid off in just over sixteen years.

There is one more amazing story from our prosperous lives that demonstrates godly prosperity when properly pursued.

Even with our scrawny earnings over the years, we were able to squirrel away some savings for each of our three children. It wasn't much. It was about $5,000 for each child, which we had always earmarked as a seed for their college education. But in our youngest daughter's junior year in high school, it seemed she was perhaps being drawn to the mission field down the road. She came home one day and said there was a three-week summer mission going to Scotland and she really believed she should go. The cost was $2,500, and she asked about using the funds we had saved for college. Barbara and I prayed about it, and we told her that our priority (and the Lord's) was always for her spiritual development. As important as college was, the Lord would have do something about that no matter what decision we made. Five thousand dollars wasn't going to go too far anyway. In light of it all, we allowed her to use those funds for that trip and another one like it the following year.

Her college fund was gone, but we were at peace with the way it was used. So when she decided to go to a private Christian college on the opposite coast from where we lived, we swallowed hard since we promised all our children that we would pay for their first year of school. After that, they were on their own. Being the last one out of the house, our well was dry, which meant we would have to take a loan to keep our word. Having prided myself on living debt-free, with the exception of a house payment and a short-term car payment, I winced

WILLIAM E. CRIPE, SR.

hard and borrowed the money. I felt like I had violated my own soul, but a promise is a promise.

About two-thirds of the way through her first year at college, we received a phone call one evening from the school. The man explained that funds had been provided by an anonymous donor to pay for our daughter's second year of school. I remember being in utter disbelief and skeptical that I wasn't being scammed in some way. As the conversation progressed, it was clear that it wasn't a scam and our daughter would be able to return the following year. But then the man added that funds had been provided to remove any other loans we might have obtained to finance her first year. As far as the rest of her education, he stated, the situation would be reviewed annually.

I was unable to speak clearly, as I was a bucket of tears. After all was said and done, our daughter had all four years of school paid for, including room and board. To this day, we do not know who the benefactor might be, but we certainly know Who was behind the benefactor's generosity.

> Seek *first* the kingdom of God and His righteousness and everything else will be added unto you.
>
> Matthew 6:33

Now you know the many reasons why this pericope from Matthew is my life passage:

> No one can serve two masters; for either he will hate the one and love the other, or he will be devoted to one and despise the other. You cannot serve God and wealth. For this reason I say to you,

do not be worried about your life, as to what you will eat or what you will drink; nor for your body, as to what you will put on. Is not life more than food, and the body more than clothing? Look at the birds of the air, that they do not sow, nor reap nor gather into barns, and yet your heavenly Father feeds them. Are you not worth much more than they? And who of you by being worried can add a single hour to his life? And why are you worried about clothing? Observe how the lilies of the field grow; they do not toil nor do they spin, yet I say to you that not even Solomon in all his glory clothed himself like one of these. But if God so clothes the grass of the field, which is alive today and tomorrow is thrown into the furnace, will He not much more clothe you? You of little faith!

Matthew 6:24–30

Every preacher, teacher, and adherent of the prosperity message who is ensnared in such a morass of destructive pap should examine themselves and their proclamations against the one and only source of true truth found in the Bible.

For the word of God is living and active and sharper than any two-edged sword, and piercing as far as the division of soul and spirit, of both joints and marrow, and able to judge the thoughts and intentions of the heart. And there is no creature hidden from His sight, but all things are open and laid bare to the eyes of Him with whom we have to do.

Hebrews 4:12–13

At the end of the day, we will each stand before the judgment seat of Christ, where, "Each man's work will become evident; for the day will show it because it is to be revealed with fire, and the fire itself will test the quality of each man's work. If any man's work which he has built on it remains, he will receive a reward" (1 Corinthians 3:13–14).

Even so, come, Lord Jesus.

ENDNOTES

Introduction

1 Joel Osteen tweet, 3/7/2011 (www.twitter.com).

Prosperity Passion in Perspective

2 Timothy Keller, *The Reason for God* (New York: Dutton), 96.

3 Dante Alighieri, *Paradiso* (Canto XXIX) (Holt, Rinehart & Winston, 1968), lines 103–108.

Pilgrimage to a Prosperity Panorama

4 Alexander Solzhenitsyn, *Gulag Archipelago II* (New York: Harper & Row, 1978).

5 http://lotterywinnerbios.blogspot.com/2009/01/ gerald-muswagon-wins-10-million-in.html

6 http://lottoreport.com/TXWinnerSuicide.htm

7 http://www.foxnews.com/story/0,2933,582119,00. html

8 Oscar Wilde, *Lady Windermere's Fan*, scene 3, pg. 49.

9 C. S. Lewis, *The Problem of Pain* (New York: MacMillan Publishing, 1962), 93.

True Prosperity Begins with the Transcendent

10 Mary Baker Eddy, *Science and Health with Key to the Scriptures* (Boston, MA: published by the trustees under the will of Mary Baker Eddy, 1934), 23.

When Prosperity and Reality Collide

11 G. Gordon Liddy, *Will* (New York: St. Martin Press, 1980).

12 Rabbi Harold Kushner, *When Bad Things Happen to Good People* (New York: Random House, 1981).

13 Philip Yancey, *Disappointment with God* (Grand Rapids: Zondervan, 1988), 179.

14 Ibid. p. 71.

The Problem of the Present Pursuit of Paradise

15 http://www.awmi.net/extra/article/healing_knowledge

16 Don Stewart, *Power and Mercy* television broadcast, February 2, 2010, 12:19 p.m. (http://www.donstewartassociation.org).

17 Ibid.

18 *New Day NRB* television broadcast, February 4, 2010.

19 *Inside Edition* television broadcast, expose of Leroy Jenkins, 3/25/2009 (http://www.insideedition.com/news/2765/terms.aspx).

20 Andrew Wommack, "Faith for Healing Is Based on Knowledge" (http://www.awmi.net/extra/article/healing_knowledge).

The Precarious Nature of Prosperity Proof Texting

21 Dr. Zachary Timmons, *New Destiny* television broadcast, February 3, 2010, 12:10 p.m.

The Predicament of the Prosperity Message

22 *Inside Edition* television broadcast, expose of Leroy Jenkins, 3/25/2009 (http://www.insideedition.com/news/2765/terms.aspx).

Pursuing a Prosperity of Truthfulness

23 Joel Osteen, *Your Best Life Now* (New York: Time Warner Book Group, 2004).

24 Timothy Keller, *The Reason for God* (New York: Dutton, 2008), 162.

25 CNN *Larry King Live*, interview with Joel Osteen, 6/20/2005 (http://transcripts.cnn.com/TRANSCRIPTS/0506/20/lki.01.html).

26 Joel Osteen, *Your Best Life Now* (New York: Time Warner Book Group, 2004), 1ff.

27 Ibid. p.3.

28 J. C. Ryle, *A Call to Holiness* (Grand Rapids: Baker Book House, 1976), 7.

There Really Is Nothing New

29 Mary Baker Eddy, *Science and Health with Key to the Scriptures* (Boston: published by the trustees under the will of Mary Baker Eddy, 1934), 111.

30 Ibid. p. 114.

31 Ibid. p. 23.

32 Joel Osteen, *Your Best Life Now* (New York: Time Warner Book Group, 2004), 13.

33 Ibid. p. 4.

34 Ibid. p. 4.

The Prosperity Gospel Needs Proper Exegesis

35 Andrew Wommack, "Faith for Healing Is Based on Knowledge" (http://www.awmi.net/extra/article/healing_knowledge).

The Prosperity Peddlers Torture the Inspired Text

36 Danette Crawford, *Joy in the Morning* television broadcast, March 10, 2010, 11:30 a.m.

37 Joel Osteen, *Your Best Life Now* (New York: Time Warner Book Group, 2004), 6.

38 Ibid. p. 18.

39 Ibid. p. 18.

40 Ibid. p. 38.

41 Ibid. p. 38.

42 Ibid. p. 80.

43 Ibid. p. 39–40.

44 Ibid. p. 40.

45 Ibid. p. 164.

The Sinking Sand of Prosperity

46 Joel Osteen, *Your Best Life Now* (New York: Time Warner Book Group, 2004), 7.

47 Ibid. p. 6.

The Proper Perspective on Prosperity

48 Philip Yancey, *Disappointment with God* (Grand Rapids: Zondervan, 1988), 80.

49 Ibid. p. 81.

50 Timothy Keller, *The Reason for God* (New York: Dutton Pub., 2008), 219.